The Self That I Long to Believe In:
The Challenge of Building Self-Esteem

By
Craig D. Lounsbrough

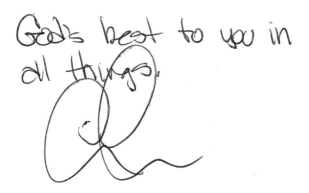

God's best to you in
all things.

For information, or to order additional copies, contact:

Beacon Publishing Group
P.O. Box 41573 Charleston, S.C. 29423
800.817.8480| beaconpublishinggroup.com

Publisher's catalog available by request.

ISBN-13: 978-1-949472-26-4

ISBN-10: 1-949472-26-4

Published in 2021. New York, NY 10001.

First Edition. Printed in the USA.

Dedication

My Mom and Dad were my greatest supporters. Sometimes that support was silent, coming in the form of a nod, a simple smile, or a sense of appreciation felt in the exchange of deep relationship. Sometimes it was more vocal, being delivered in a comment, a card, or something said in a special moment and held close long after that moment. In it all there was a belief in us that encouraged us when we did not believe in us.

Therefore, this book is dedicated to Dave and Donna Lounsbrough. Although you have both long passed, your influence has not. When my self-esteem wanes or it finds itself attacked by myself or someone else, I lean back in time and pick up your words once again. And in that I am refreshed and restored. Therefore, this book is dedicated to both of you for without you it could not have been written.

I also dedicate this book to my two ever-astounding children, Cheyenne and Corey. I watch within both of you a sense of strength and courage that people my age envy. I watch both of you call up a resolute sense of self to engage the realities of a world less than welcoming and even less than encouraging. I wish that I had your courage and self-esteem when the world comes at me in those same ways.

Above all, this book is dedicated to the God who inspired the concept and guided the shaping of it. Over the many years that these articles were penned and over the many months that they came together in the process of writing this book there were innumerable moments when the right words, the perfect phrase, or an entirely fresh idea came out of nowhere. At these moments, I found myself completely cognizant of the fact that something other than myself was writing. I realized that in reality I am not an author. I am just a corroborator of the least sort. Therefore, may God use this book in service of His Kingdom in whatever manner He deems appropriate.

Table of Contents

Introduction

I can only imagine how much low self-esteem has robbed us as individuals and ransacked our culture. It is a rogue beast bent on diminishing us to some point of forlorn incapacity. Plagued by this beast, we live out marginalized lives that surrender the accomplishments and forsake the achievements that could have been ours. We grope through this existence, meagerly living out each day by surviving, rather than realizing that we can live with an intensity that will have caused the day to finish having survived us.

Low self-esteem has been a thread I have observed throughout my many years of serving people. It is no respecter of persons, pillaging people of every race, socio-economic standing, and cultural niche. It runs rogue through the human race, not being deterred by the greatest of achievements, the most profound wealth, or the loftiest social standing achievable. We are all susceptible. And likely, we are all victims.

We can theorize and formulate creative solutions to counter or possibly eliminate low self-esteem. Or we can create trite and rather self-soothing ideas to calm souls ravaged by the plague of self-hatred. But instead of all of that, we might be wise to get down to ground level, stand eye-to-eye with this malignant issue, and in doing so understand both what it is and what it is not. Then we might want to call it out, speak something practically potent into it, and wrestle it into submission on its own turf. That's what this book does.

Strategically, the first two chapters of this book are dedicated to the idea of new beginnings. That may not sound revelatory. However, unless we believe that we are worth a new beginning, the rest of the book doesn't matter. For many of us, we feel that we aren't worth a new 'anything.' Therefore, to effectively explore the concepts outlined in this book and to embrace them out of some sense of rightful ownership, we must believe that things can be new. We must believe that where we are is a place, not a prison. That our view of ourselves is not bound to anything other than the people and the events who reinforced what we are not. We must believe that tomorrow will not be today in rerun. For then, we are positioned to change.

Once the foundational idea that change is both possible and doable has been established, the issue of low self-esteem is then addressed from a variety of perspectives that are common contributors. Low self-esteem is carefully addressed in terms of the variant ways that we attempt to deal with it. Most of these approaches are rooted in cultural methodologies that are flawed, inadequate and shaped by the deteriorating nature of society. Additionally, self-esteem is addressed by looking at the individual with a depth and an acumen that practically evidences the profound nature of our individual humanity. As a means to build out that reality, the capability of our humanity is also drawn out and rigorously expounded upon in terms of what achievements are actually possible. Finally, all of this is brought together in the conclusion to provide an inspirational capstone to the overall content of the book.

This book is a combination of thirty-nine years of walking with a nearly innumerable number of people who found themselves bent under the weight of self-hatred. Over these years, I have written a large number of articles and blogs on this difficult and paralyzing issue. This book is a thoughtfully expanded and enriched collection of this material, carefully and meticulously brought into book format. The chapters are unapologetically practical, speaking to people not in some theoretical format, for that does very little for people who are hurting.

Rather, this book speaks into the darkness of their pain and the hopelessness of their vision for themselves. This book is written out of the hope that something said will strike the reader sufficiently for them to pick up the thought and work it into and against the darkness of their self-hatred. This is a book to lift people. A book to encourage people. A book to give them a handful of workable thoughts and a reliable road out of the low self-esteem that has dogged their days and darkened their lives. And if perchance I can do that for someone, the energy and time invested in writing this book will have been well-spent.

Craig D. Lounsbrough

Chapter One
A New Start
The Concept of a New Beginning

"Against all hope, Abraham in hope believed and so became the father of many nations, just as it had been said to him, 'So shall your offspring be.'"
- Romans 4:18 (NIV)

"You may have a fresh start any moment you choose, for this thing that we call 'failure' is not the falling down, but the staying down."
- Mary Pickford

Believing in New Beginnings
The word 'imperative' can be intimidating. It's a tersely demanding word and we by nature shy away from demands of this sort. However, without abusing the word, it is 'imperative' that we believe in the possibility of new beginnings. For if we don't believe in new beginnings we have closed the door to all the new beginnings that stand poised and at the ready just on the other side of that door. If we don't believe in new beginnings, we have said that we don't believe in life. But maybe more pointedly, we have said that we don't believe in ourselves.

For many of us, the crippling nature of our low self-esteem has long destroyed our ability to believe in ourselves. As such, we are unable to believe that we have sufficient value to warrant a

1

new beginning. For if we cannot believe that new beginnings are possible for us or that we are in some remote way deserving of them, everything that follows in the book that you are holding will be interpreted as a collection of nice ideas that might warm the heart and challenge the mind, but they will utterly fail to change your life. This book then will have failed for the single reason that we allowed it to.

Therefore, at the outset I would ask that we would be willing to entertain the idea that new beginnings exist, even if we don't see them as existing for ourselves. That life was created with ample space for new beginnings. That the entirety of existence itself is created upon, built around and has been perpetuated by new beginnings in such a way that without them existence itself would cease to exist. And if we are unable to embrace that reality as existing for us, may we at the outset at least acknowledge that new beginnings do exist.

The Struggle to Believe

Some of us don't believe in new beginnings because we've been brutalized by life in such a way that new beginnings have become the stuff of cruel myth. Some of us have watched our dreams obliterated to the point that dreaming itself is just a dream. We've witnessed the curt dissolution of our marriages and the violent collapse of our families within which all of our new beginnings had been trustingly and tenderly packaged. Jobs vanished with no warning, dragging dreams down into some abyss that was deeper than the reach of our hope. Terminal illnesses squashed futures, abandoning us to the regret of a past we now have no time to correct. A child sits writhing in detox when only a handful of years ago they sat on our laps enraptured in stories of princesses and fairytale wonderment. Whatever tragedies have befallen us, they have destroyed our sense of worth and have seared a charred realism within us that leaves no room for the hope of new beginnings.

Renovations and Their Purpose

On the other side, we might believe in new beginnings but we've confused the reality of new beginnings with slick make-overs and tedious revisions. Or, since we don't believe in new beginnings for ourselves, we've replaced them with revisions and renovations so that we have something that looks new. Renovation is quite deceptive as it looks to be something convincingly new when it's nothing more than something old, cleverly veneered. We see it as new because we've surrendered to the fear that 'new' in the purest sense of the word doesn't exist, at least for us. And so we've opted for a bit of 'nip-n-tuck' or a vigorous spit-shine so that something 'old' in our lives has the appearance of being something 'new' in order to hide the disappointment of a life ever old and never new. However, God said, "I am making all things new" (Revelation 21:5, NIV). I must say that I'm not hearing any renovation in that.

If we push those renovations aside, we are either left with the stunning, nearly improbable reality of new beginnings, or the hopelessness that new beginnings are not in the cards for us. If we abandon the pursuit of renovations, we will either believe in new beginnings or we will fall haplessly victim to a life of endless endings. All of that is terribly risky. And so, we tend to stick to renovation because it's a safer bet.

New Beginnings as Out of Reach

We often tend to shy away from the idea of new beginnings because the scope of them often exceeds the degree of our bravery, or the extent of our abilities, or the reach of our faith, or the degree of our worth. Are we sufficiently stalwart to abandon the definable comforts of the familiar for the trackless frontier of all that is new? Can we abandon control of such a lofty journey so that in our fear we don't irreverently cram all that is new back into the confines of all that was old so that what is new dies at the hands of our cowardice? Most profoundly, can we believe that we, in fact, are worth a new beginning like this? For if we are not, such speculation is a waste of time spent and dreams dreamt that will die in the dreaming.

Therefore, whether it's a seared realism, or an apprehensive fear, or a poor view of oneself, we must move our hearts and our minds to a position where they can at least embrace the possibility of new beginnings. If we can at least accept the 'idea' of a new beginning, even if it is from an emotional distance because we cannot as of yet see it for ourselves, we can at least begin there. And if we can do that, we have then set the stage for phenomenal things to actually unfold in our lives.

The Chemistry of New Beginnings

So, what would we actually do with a new start, if it were possible? I mean a really new, 'new' start? Not something that looks new because we've vigorously buffed something that's old and caressed its finish to a new luster. Not some radical make-over of something that's radically old so that it looks convincingly new. Not a tedious and meticulous restoration that's going to erase the footprints of time and grant something old a few more years of life until it looks old again. Not history in reprise, or worn ideas given fresh soles so that they might eke out a few more miles.

Our definition of 'new' has become crippled to a sour limp by our paralyzing fear of failure. It has become tamed to a docile death by the soothing rub of mediocrity that is calming when the unknown is not. Bound by a chafing sense of personal inadequacy that stalks our deepest dreams, we have opted to let those dreams die that we might preserve familiarity and kill risk. We let the imposing hedge shaped of cultural expectations, the foreboding fence constructed of social norms, and our own egregious lack of self-confidence cause us to abandon anything new in a soiled trade for things accepted within hedge and fence and fears. This is not life. Whether we feel ourselves deserving of life or not, still this is not life.

New is not a revision or a recalibration. It is not an adjustment, a manner of tweaking, a bit of nip and tuck, or some creative remodeling. It is a vision cast out beyond 'what is' that sees 'what is' as a pivotal launching point to 'what can be.' Vision will break the bonds of 'what is,' because it is within the 'what is' that vision itself will be broken if it remains in that place. Vision trades a revisionist mentality for an explorer's vitality. It is boldness untethered and raw courage let loose to run. It shrewdly builds on the past, but it is not a prisoner shackled to it nor does it sense an obligation to stay there even though a chorus of visionless voices in opposition might say so. And it is here that we need to abandon what new is not and embrace what it is.

Such ideas are certainly challenging, particularly when we struggle with issues of self-esteem. They can be frightening, leaving us with a sense that a new beginning of anything is leagues beyond our reach. However, as a means of considering the possibilities of a new beginning for you, I would encourage you to think through the following:

First, A New Future is Built from the Raw Materials of the Past

The nature of life is such that we plan for the future with the past shaping the nature of our plans. That's just natural. We build for tomorrow on the foundation of the past because, for good or ill, the past is what we've got. The past holds the raw material from which futures are built. The memories, experiences, wounds, trauma, gains, losses and various lessons of the past are the natural fodder that feeds a future seeking sustenance to foster its growth and fuel its pioneering expansion.

Oddly enough, we might want to consider the fact that the things that have run roughshod over our self-esteem are the very raw materials from which great futures are constructed. The more the damage, the more the material and therefore the greater the opportunities. The future cannot help but be shaped, built and ultimately fed by the past. The worse the past, the greater the feeding. However, in all the shaping and building and feeding, the future does not need to 'be' the past, nor can it be.

However, because the past was painful we presume that the future will be as well. We assume that if we build with the raw materials of a past fashioned by pain, molded by heartache, and rubbed raw with rejection, the future will be a mirror image of all the stuff that we don't want to see in any mirror. And in embracing this belief, we want nothing to do with the past but at the same we realize that we can't run from it. It shapes us whether we like it or not. It's the material that we have to work with regardless of how much we abhor it. It's not going anywhere. So if we're making a future out of that kind of stuff, it can only be bad.

But what we fail to realize is that it's the painful stuff that makes for the best futures. It's the lessons learned in the pain. It's the tenacity that grows strong in the angst of the struggle. It's the knowledge that we develop a deeper understanding of life when we're walking through the darkness. It's the wisdom that we gain in the wrestling. The insight that we develop in the isolation. The feelings that we come to understand only by weathering trials that we don't. This is the raw material, the precious raw material. And it has a potency and a power that we completely underestimate and recklessly discount. This stuff builds the best futures.

Second, a New Future Demands Risk
If our self-esteem is low, risk is not our friend. At those moments when we find the idea of a new future as unexpectedly tantalizing and a bit electrifying, we begin to hem and haw because we start realizing the rather steep risks involved in developing a new future. It means believing that a future exists to be

believed in. It means exercising some degree of faith that this future will be different this time when it has not been different any other time. It means placing this already shaky sense of self at great peril. It means making ourselves horrifyingly vulnerable to a future that we're not certain exists, and if perchance it does, it's trusting that it will treat us well once we get there. And finally, it's realizing that if we embark on this frightening journey, there's no coming back.

But when our self-confidence has been beaten to a pulp, every risk looks big. There is no little risk. Risk is risk, and it's formidable regardless of the nature of it. Risk is blatantly hazardous because it can be fickle, lending no sense of security as to what it will do with us. In a way it's slippery. It can turn rogue in a heartbeat. It's the worst of our fears unleashed because it can take us to the worst of places. But risk is the invitation to greater things, not the barrier to them. It's a fact of life that we must embrace if we are to move forward in the face of life.

But we have to think about the risk in *not* going forward. We have to consider the risk of staying where we are and remaining who we are. We have to ponder the price that we will pay for being apathetic versus pressing against our apathy and taking a shot at something better. We may not have the confidence that the future will be good, but neither do we have the certainty that it will be bad. Maybe not to risk is the greatest risk of all. So, we must weigh the risk in acting or not acting and in doing so ask which is the greater risk.

Third, a New Future Will Demand Something New

A new future cannot be entirely crafted from old material. Recycling is a great thing. Yet, our past can only be recycled so much. Everything that we recycle is limited to and constrained by the raw material that makes it up. We can possess a boundless imagination and couple that imagination with a wildly creative mind in repurposing the stuff of our past. Yet, the raw material that we work with will create limitations because the materials themselves are limited. If we have come to believe that we are not worth a new beginning, we possess no legitimate rationale to attempt anything new. Therefore, all we've got to work with is the old stuff. And while we can be ingeniously creative with it, creativity will soon turn sour without something new to refresh it.

If we want a truly new 'new' future, something about it must be new. 'New' implies something that does not possess any of the elements that we already possess. Something must be added that has not been added before. Some place that we have never been must be some place that we're now willing to consider going. Some direction that we've either adamantly avoided or never thought to consider needs to be considered and mapped out, even if we initially embark upon it in thought only. Some decision that we may have avoided out of the fear that it may rock our world may need to be made and be granted permission to rock our world a bit, knowing that sometimes it's the rocking that brings the changing.

But it's the inclusion of the 'new' that interjects a fresh and unsullied dynamic. In the midst of our dread apprehension about anything new, we need to understand that something 'new' can be subtle. It can be small. It can be that toe in the water instead of the all-out plunge. A little 'new' can go a remarkably long way. And as we rather tentatively think about something new, we need to understand that just a touch of 'new' can gently nudge the trajectory of our lives by the slightest of margins but still break the worst of our cycles.

Fourth, a New Future Means Grieving What We're Leaving

Leaving something behind is one thing. But what we don't consider is the grieving in the leaving. When we leave something behind it will naturally leave a hole of some sort. Whether that hole be large or small, disorienting or desired, painful or painless, it is the now vacant space that was once occupied by whatever it is that we're leaving. Creating a space creates a measure of discomfort because we're not used to a hole being where something else used to be. On top of that, we're naturally prone to fill empty spaces for the simple fact that they're empty. 'Empty' doesn't mean that something's wrong. It means that something's coming. And because what has come before has been painful at times, that doesn't mean that it will be this time.

A low self-esteem is the belief that we carry because of the holes that we have. Whether those holes are made up of something we've lost, or something that we should have had but never did. Whatever the case, we are a prolific collection of holes strewn across the landscape of our lives that broadcast our inadequacy. Our holes hold out our deficits in bold relief. They tell us everything that we're not because of everything that should have been in those holes. They tell us that we weren't worth the few things that we accidently did have, which explains why they were taken, leaving more holes than we can count in the taking. They convince us that we're a collection of holes because holes are what we deserve. But what we need to understand is that holes are a part of our journey, not a commentary on our value.

Sometimes the pain of accepting the hole is greater than the pain of the thing that once occupied the hole. In the ensuing emotional trade-off that we find ourselves embroiled in, we often take the very thing that was removed from the hole and attempt to put it back in order to fill in the hole and stop the pain. The problem is that the nature of both the hole and the thing that we've removed have changed in the removing because the removed item wasn't supposed to go back. It no longer fits because it's not supposed to. Leaving the past means grieving the past, not attempting to put the proverbial round peg in what is now a square hole.

Fifth, a New Future is Not Building a Museum

We have this prevailing hoarding tendency. We simply like collecting stuff because it feels like all of this 'stuff' grounds us when our lives are spiraling so wildly that nothing's grounding us. We recognize the need to move on and we understand that we need to leave the past behind as we move on. We know that. But despite the often immense problems that the old stuff created for us, the old stuff grounds us as we deal with the bit of shifting that happens before the new 'stuff' is sufficiently developed to ground us.

So, we want to keep a few mementos. We want to grab a handful of assorted trinkets and knick-knacks to have something to ground us in the certainty of days gone-by, even though we wish that the pain associated with them would go 'bye.' However, too often keeping a few mementos turns into keeping a whole lot of mementos. Eventually, we're leaning toward creating a memento museum. Before long, we've managing a museum. And soon thereafter, we're living in it. We not supposed to live in it because it wasn't designed for that purpose. As we noted previously, this is the rich raw material from which we craft a future, not the raw material that we use to preserve our past. However, we want to sort and catalog and categorize and organize and stow and store all that stuff. And before we know it, the museum is managing us because our self-esteem constantly yells that we have no ability to manage a new future.

This is not to say that we shouldn't preserve our past as a sacred part of our journey. Indeed, we need to both remember and honor the past. However, when we set about creating museums, the task becomes so monstrous that we end up living in the museum that we've created. Or worse yet, it ends up living in us. When we do that, our future has become about preserving our past. Although we confuse the two, we need to understand that honoring the past is far different than living in it.

A New Future
We were not born into a world of immense and improbable possibilities just to be chained to the disillusioning limits of finite possibilities. We have a God who says that the impossible is just a rumor. It would behoove us to understand that that statement is not conditional as if it applies to a select few, but not us. We can remove ourselves from such an incredible promise, but we cannot remove the promise in the removing.

14

If we want a really new 'new' start, we'd be wise to realize that the idea of what has been will always be only 'be,' if we choose it to be. And in the oddity of life, we have the power and privilege to decide either way. In essence, we must forgo historical face-lifts and be willing to risk. We must be bold enough to incorporate something entirely new and we must grieve with a firm intent the hole of things left behind. We need to hold the past close to our hearts, but we must refuse to build museums around it. And if we can begin this process, even if that be a slight first step, the next things we must tackle may be the most difficult thing of all … and that is our belief in our ability to do these very things.

The Hard Questions:
1. Which is your biggest fear, letting something go or anticipating something new?
2. Ask yourself why you fear either of these. Is the reason that you fear them substantial enough to cause the level of fear that you're feeling?
3. Dealing with fear is not about resolving it. Rather, it's about finding the courage to push through it. What is one thing you can do to begin to develop that courage?

Chapter Two
Beginnings
An End is Only a Beginning in Disguise

"'See, I am doing a new thing! Now it springs up; do you not perceive it? I am making a way in the wilderness and streams in the wasteland.'"
-   Isaiah 43:19 (NIV)

"Every new beginning comes from some other beginning's end."
-   Seneca

Both the character and the enormity of some endings are such that the loss we've experienced often leaves us believing that the ending is so final that there is nothing beyond it for any sort of beginning to get a foothold. We stand before endings that are so crushing and whose girth is so unfathomably massive that they become definitive in and of themselves. They are indisputably conclusive. They are the final 'final' statement. There is nothing after endings such as these because there is nothing left to be left. Therefore, endings are not just unfathomable. They become entirely irrefutable.

When it comes to self-esteem, it's losses like these that crush us. It's experiencing defeats that are of such gravity that any victories beyond the defeats

16

feel wildly incomprehensible. We come to believe that defeats are our lot in life, and as such they are the final word. They are the definitive period at the end of the sentence. They are the conclusion of what is now a forever conclusion. And as such, there is no room for any new beginning because everything behind us that we might have crafted one from was destroyed. Therefore, while the losses methodically erode our self-confidence, the belief that the losses are patently unredeemable renders the erosion a forever fixture of our failed lives.

Over time, a battered self-esteem comes to see life as a litany of irreparable losses. The crushing mass of our perceived personal deficits are so crippling that our ability to craft new beginnings (much less sustain them should they actually happen) is perceived as impossible. Life is not about new beginnings. It is about a journey of surviving old losses. It's not about looking forward. It's about avoiding looking anywhere for fear that looking at the past would be too painful and looking into the future would be too disappointing.

But every now and then we're compelled to take a peek at the horizon ahead of us. But as soon as we do, we immediately recoil from any fanciful thoughts of journeying to it because we assume that if we got there we'd just fall off of it anyway. What we don't understand is that a horizon is not something to fall off of. It's not an end. It's not a

17

conclusion. It's not a period at the end of some sentence in the story of your life. Rather, a horizon is a horizon only because there's something on the other side of it that makes it a horizon. No ending possesses the power to make a horizon something without another side. And maybe that 'something' that's on the other side is your new beginning.

Endings Start as Beginnings

If we're honest with ourselves we know that endings are the product of some new start that played itself out in whatever way it did until it become an ending. So, at some point we had a new beginning; otherwise we wouldn't be experiencing this ending. Something might be concluding, but it's only doing so because at some point it started. However, by their very nature, we don't believe that endings possess anything to generate a new start because they ended. They're done. They're gone.

Clearly, endings are not beginnings. But they set the perfect stage for them. Because endings are happening right now and beginnings have yet to begin, endings require that we believe that they are only a small part of a much larger story that's already written out on a page that's already started to turn. We just don't see that part of the book yet.

Therefore, if we have solidified our perception of endings as being nothing more than endings, we will have effectively barred the majority of beginnings from ever coming even remotely close to our lives. If by chance one sneaks in, our shattered self-esteem tends to label it as a fluke. If one inadvertently happens, we sabotage it because it can't really be real anyway. Or we turn our backs on it because it apparently showed up in the wrong place and so we let it perish in some shadowy corner of our darkened existence. Subsequently, the tempo and tenor of our lives will be perpetually cut short by the loss involved in endings, versus being eternally cut free by the anticipation of beginnings that lay staged in every ending.

If such a theme persists over a sufficient period of time, we will be beset by such cancerous maladies as depression, anxiety, pessimism, and a host of other debilitating attitudes that will cast our lives in tones of drizzling cold gray. In time, we will rather effectively validate our conviction that there are no new beginnings because we thwarted every single one of them. The page turned, but we weren't there to read it. Therefore, our self-sabotaging behaviors will leave us achingly barren of new beginnings and crushed to desperation by the belief that the beginning that might soothe the pain of our endings will never begin. And in it all, our worthlessness is reinforced at our own hands.

The Nature of Beginnings and Endings
In reality, there are many times when we welcome endings. Without question, there are a whole lot of

things that we just can't wait to wash our hands of. We all have those nagging situations that we desperately wish would give us blessed relief by vanishing altogether. Sometimes we can't wait for the day to end, or for that looming deadline to pass, or for a particular event to be mercifully over. There are some endings that we joyously welcome with open arms, and by the time they arrive we find ourselves ecstatic that whatever's done is finally done. Nonetheless, despite these periodically ecstatic moments, our aversion to endings remains doggedly resolute.

Endings can be incapacitating and painful for an unfathomable range of reasons, most of which we never come close to identifying because we're too ensnared in the loss to see anything but the loss. We don't really identify what we're actually doing with whatever the ending is, or what the ending is actually doing to us, because we're too 'lost in the loss' to even begin to consider any of that. We're normalizing the loss as being our norm or we're justifying it as being the way that fate always shows up. Therefore, we can't see anything in the loss that we can harness in the service of what's about to begin because we're too caught up in that loss. We become lost in the loss. Therefore, this generous collection of rich resources and ever-expanding insights that were designed to maximize our new beginning are left to perish in the backwaters of an ending of which these things were not supposed to be a part.

And so, without remedy or hope thereof, the ending we are experiencing razes us flat. From this immobilizing point, any vision of a tomorrow is swallowed whole by the singular vision of the end that has beset us and the loss that has betrayed us. And because the loss is all that we can see, the ending becomes an end in itself when, directly ahead of us, new beginnings are being forged and fresh byways are being laid out from the very ending that has consumed us. We're simply too lost in the loss to see what stands but a mere step away or what lies within the turn of a single page.

The Seeds of a New Beginning

Because this occurs, we're left with the inability to see within the loss the liberally scattered seeds of a fresh beginning. We've lost the ability to comprehend that an end is always a beginning. We have recklessly exchanged the circular splendor of life for the arresting voice of fear that declares 'circular' as the muse of weaker minds. In doing so, we have forsaken the emancipating ability to fathom that whatever is ending for us is always more than an ending. And we would be wise to consider that without that ability, we will forever live the endless tale of endless endings that was anything but the story that God originally penned for us.

Such endings rob us of the vision (and the elemental conviction borne of such a vision) that things are escorted out of our lives so that better things have room to be escorted in. The awareness that death relentlessly begets life slips deeper into some murky cognizance of the cycle of life progressively abandoned. Rather than seeing life as an opportunist that persistently stands ready to build something out of the smoldering ashes and raise something up out of the tangled carnage, we are mired in the dreary fantasy of irresponsible idealism or the fate predetermined for losers such as ourselves. And in embracing such views, we begin to see the whole of existence itself as held haplessly captive to the very same forces and the very same fate that we ourselves face. And if life itself is hamstrung in just the same way that we are, how can there be any hope for anything?

While it takes very little imagination to conceptualize life as drowning in loss, it takes far more to see it as brimming with beginnings. In such a terribly fragile exchange, the sense that an end is only a beginning in disguise slips between our fingers and drains from the crevices of our souls. The fact of improbable new beginnings as being stitched into the very fabric of life becomes the fiction of what is purported as fact. It becomes the pathetic story of those who can't face the reality of this sordid existence of ours. Subsequently, we are left to wallow in the impoverished lie that life steals with no inkling any blessing that stands ready to sweep in in the exchange.

And so, how do we learn to see a beginning being formed in the ashes of whatever end we've experienced? How do we begin to look beyond the reality of the ending that stands looming over us to see the new beginning that stands a mere step away from us? We might do that better by getting some obstructive thinking out of the way:

First, How Our Loss is Shaped

What we're prone to do is visualize the loss within the agenda that we had created for that thing, or that person, or that life-phase. Everything in our lives is assigned some place or position, whether we realize that we've created that assignment or not. That placement is based on our determination as to how this person or this thing should be interacting with our lives. At some rudimentary level, we have a general awareness of this role as we've assigned it. However, it's not until we've incurred this loss that we recognize the full extent of its role. At times, the loss of the role exceeds the actual loss of the person or the thing, thereby leaving us confused, disoriented and wondering why we were hit so hard.

Because of that unrecognized role, we've not recognized a larger role that's simply playing itself out so it can play other things in. We assign a role to these things or these people, but we often don't assign a length of time for that role. We assume they will always be around. We grant them some sense of unrealistic permanence. We create a life that's fixed instead of fluid. Therefore, we lose the sense that life allows certain things to pass in order to make room for new things that will play new roles. However, that was not how we had planned it all out.

Second, We Don't Want to Lose Something
Quite simply, we tend to hate endings because many of our endings involve things that we don't want to lose. Certainly, there are many things that we're glad to be rid of, but many times some 'thing,' or some person, or some life-phase played such a potent role in our lives that we simply can't imagine going on without it. Or we feel that the end of this 'thing' has come far too prematurely, like some predatory thief having long stalked us in heartless silence, leaving us bereft of everything we could have gotten out of this thing, or it out of us.

In many cases, we had stitched that person or that thing or that success into our lives with such precise seamlessness that what was meant to be a gift to be enjoyed became a part of who we were. Often, we rob things of their true worth by granting them a place that they were never meant to have, or a position they were never meant to occupy. We made these things what they were not shaped to be and therefore our expectations of the role that they were supposed to play don't match the loss of the role that we forced them to play. If we had let them be what they were intended to be, our view of those

24

things and the loss of them would be quite different, likely radically different.

Whatever the case, we've been cheated, or short-changed, or short-sheeted in some manner that elicits a sense of bewildering and entirely unjust loss. To complicate matters, such supposedly premature and inappropriate losses elicit a gyrating spectrum of destabilizing emotions that compound the confusion of the loss. The loss becomes more about the fact that it shouldn't have happened rather than the fact that it did.

Third, We Fear That Whatever We've Lost Can Never Be Replaced

There's the rather paralyzing fear that what we've lost is so unique or so precisely suited to our lives that it can never be replaced. There's an immediate sense that losing something demands that it be replaced...immediately. Or better yet, we somehow expect that something should have shown up before the loss happened so that the replacement is immediate and seamless. There's that sense where we don't want to disturb the continuity of our lives and the fixed rhythm that we've created. Things have been disrupted, sometimes dramatically so, and we want to stop the disruption by instantly replacing whatever it was that we lost. We're caught up in the ever-accelerating fear that maybe it can't be replaced. Maybe there is no substitution. Maybe there is nothing to swap it out with, and we will therefore have to settle with the disruption of a forever "new normal" that we have absolutely no interest in or find appalling.

What we tend to miss is that replacement only serves to perpetuate the repetition of the past instead of realizing that creating space for something new creates space for something fresh. As unsettling as they might be, transitions are a move toward something better, not a lifestyle of something worse or a dulling perpetuation of what was. And it is out of something fresh that this journey of ours is so often refreshed when it would otherwise become repugnantly stagnant.

Fourth, Glorifying the End
If the nature of life is such that we are forced to tolerate endings, we want them to be good or even glorious. If it has to happen, we want an end to have some meaning to it; that whatever is ending was significant or possibly spectacular while it was around. If something's going to end and we can't stop it, we want to send it off with some sort of recognition, or with some degree of pomp, or with a rich flush of appreciation, or a final 'hurrah' of the most robust sort. If there's going to be an ending, we want it to be one that will be such an ending that it will never be forgotten. We can't hold on to that which we're losing, but we can make the end grand and glorious to the point that the memory of it all will always stay with us. There's nothing inherently

wrong about bringing something to a close in a manner that's respectful and celebratory, unless this becomes our one and total focus.

Consequently, the loss becomes about glorifying the end so as to ignore the loss or offset the injustice of it. We can't deny the loss, but we can shift our focus to something a whole lot less painful. We can eke out something that we can live with because anything else we feel we will die from. So let's make it grand and then move on with our lives letting that be the whole of our memory.

Fifth, We Fear That an Ending Might Be a Failure

What if the ending was really a failure? What if whatever it was that ended wasn't really supposed to end, but it did because somebody screwed up somewhere? What if this really wasn't the time at all? What if this loss really was grossly premature and achingly unnecessary? What if this loss was due to our stupidity or poor timing or lack of insight or lackluster commitment? What if this loss was the product of someone else's blatant failure, or a glorious manifestation of ignorance in all its ignorant glory?

Sometimes losses are so unexplainable and seemingly irrational that we think this way because we can't reason it out any other way. The fact is, given the apparent senselessness of so many losses, it doesn't seem reasonable that we can think beyond this kind of thinking. And it may well be that the loss did not have to happen and maybe it should not have happened at all. Face it, we live in a fallen world. Yet, life is plenty big enough and it has ample room to take the most tragic mistakes and weave them into the most wonderful of opportunities if we let it do so. An ending is only a failure if we choose not to tease out the manifold lessons in the ending. Therefore, if the ending was a failure it was likely a product of the fact that we did not tease out those lessons.

Sixth, We Fear That There Will Be No New Beginning

So, what if this is an end and nothing more than an end? What if nothing emerges from whatever it is that we've lost? What if life doesn't go on, or there are no opportunities beyond this, or it all dies right here? Could an end be irrevocably an end where a beginning of any kind simply does not exist? Is there a place where life stops because there is absolutely nothing else ahead? Could this be that dreaded chasm where there is no other side from which to pick up the journey? Could the 'end of it all' now actually be the end of it all?

And it is this very fear that makes most of our endings so terribly frightening. We often wonder will the road run out, will an irrevocable end eventually come, and will there be no place to go because the future simply won't exist and the past is

28

forever gone? Is that where we finally stand? And could it be that this place of a forever 'nevermore' is where we will now forever stand? Yet, it is looking at the nature and fabric of life, and in the looking realizing that things always find a way to go forward because there is always a place to go forward to. Always.

An End as a Beginning in Disguise

Life is a relentless perpetuation of things arising out of things that have passed. There is the coming and the going. The emptying out and the filling up. The uprooting and the planting. There is an unrelenting exchange that makes things unrelentingly new. It is much like the coming of spring which heralds a titanic resurgence arising out of the debris and decay of fall. It is a message woven into the most intimate fabric of creation where nothing ends because an end is only a beginning in disguise.

It's living with the understanding that loss is real, and that loss can be utterly devastating. But loss is only a precursor to something that will step in and grant us a new vantage point from which to visualize a new future. It might be different. It could take us in an entirely new direction. It may well be unfamiliar. However, it is the next step picking up where the previous step left off. And whatever the nature of this new step might be, life is such that it opens new horizons, paints new vistas, and calls us to perpetual adventure if we're willing to heed the call. An ending is only a beginning in disguise. And the negative view of ourselves will never be powerful enough to offset the reality that these beginnings are yours just as much as they are everyone else's.

To embrace what follows in these pages you must be able to 'entertain' the belief that you are worth new beginnings. This book is about a new beginning in your life. And so, to 'entertain' the idea that you can have one is the first step toward believing that you actually can. Your endings are only your beginnings in disguise. Your beginnings lie in the pages ahead.

The Hard Questions:
1. Pick an ending in your life that you've not been able to get past. Take a minute and ask yourself what kind of beginning could possibly come out of this ending?
2. Once you've determined what kind of beginning could come out of this ending, ask yourself if you want to deal with the pain and the work that may result in birthing this new beginning?
3. If you're up for it, what would the first step be to actually begin cultivating this new beginning?

Craig D. Lounsbrough

Chapter Three

Our Identity and Value
Internal Not External

"In the day when God created man, He made him in the likeness of God. He created them male and female, and He blessed them and named them Man in the day when they were created."
- Genesis 5:1-2 (NIV)

"Three kinds of souls, three prayers:

1) I am a bow in your hands, Lord. Draw me, lest I rot.

2) Do not overdraw me, Lord. I shall break.

3) Overdraw me, Lord, and who cares if I break."

- Nikos Kazantzakis

We're driven. Whether that's for our good or our ill, we're driven. That drive may be born of a free spirit bent on living with unimpeded freedom, or it might be a drive used to hold ourselves captive. It might be a drive to face ourselves, or a drive to run from ourselves. We can be driven to do great things,

31

or to hide from great things. Being driven grants us the ability to fly, but we can use it just as readily to die.

If we are bent under the weight of a low self-esteem, our drive is often exercised to our own demise. It's used to create places to hide, excuses to run, rationalizations to justify the awful person that we are not, and the freedom to embrace beliefs about ourselves that have no basis in reality other than the reality we've crafted from the skewed messages of others. On the other hand, we might become driven to prove ourselves as worthy through various accomplishments and achievements. We work, we strive, we reach, and we relentlessly press on to show that we are more than what we've come to believe ourselves to be. If we fail in such an endeavor, we're driven to convince ourselves that we are nothing of the sort so that we don't ever take on such a preposterous task ever again. Either way, we possess a drive even if it isn't used in our best interest.

Driven to Prove Our Worth
Maybe this whole mentality of drive has been a product of our life story, having to do it all ourselves because no one was there to help us. Maybe this left us with the need to prove ourselves and to establish our worth by whatever means necessary. Often we have the need to display our intellectual prowess, to

exercise the muscle of our skill-set or to flaunt our expertise in order to secure our place in some sort of ill-defined and vague pecking order that defines our sense of worth and value. Our identity then becomes entirely defined by all of the things that we do to prove our worth and the efforts that we put forth in doing them.

In some instances this happens because we've lived in someone's shadow and we need to show ourselves as bigger than the shadow that was cast upon us, or at least prove that we're as big as whoever shadow that was. At other times we're out to prove people wrong, to conclusively show beyond any shadow of a doubt that we're competent even though people repeatedly said we were entirely incompetent. It can be the product of a deeply ingrained behavioral pattern where we grew up being affirmed when we performed, with such affirmation being clearly withheld when we didn't. In the end, it's typically ourselves that we're really trying to convince simply because the toughest audience that we play to is 'us.'

Driven to Prove Our Lack of Worth
Or we've done the opposite of all of this by being driven to surrender to minimums. We've decided to withdraw from it all and just do what we need to do to get to the next day. It's about being driven to draw away and hide so that others won't see us for who we are and thereby judge us, or we won't see them and

subsequently judge ourselves by comparison. We're driven not to be driven so that we avoid failure, or anything might even remotely resemble failure. Or, we're often driven to surrender before the battle ever shows up so that surrender was a choice and not a pathetic manifestation of our inabilities to fight the battle.

In embracing this mentality, we're not driven to disprove this sense of worthlessness. Rather, we're driven to prove it by not disproving it. It's a battle of a different sort. It's not a surrendering to any battle that we've fought. To the contrary, it's a surrendering to the need to fight for something that doesn't exist to be fought for. Surrender then indisputably evidences our worthlessness while simultaneously granting us full license to walk away without guilt or remorse. And while such a package seems marvelously relieving, it is in fact horribly life-killing.

The Failure of Trying to Proving Ourselves Proving Our Worthlessness

The drive to prove ourselves is wildly relentless. But what are we trying to prove and in what way are we trying to prove it? If we wish to prove ourselves as inadequate or inferior, we do so by acting in ways that substantiate those things. Our lives become a reflexive response to the preconceived notion that we are worthless. Therefore, our actions reinforce what we have come to believe ourselves to be.

34

We can sabotage our own good fortune. We can take opportunity and destroy it, thereby declaring that it was never really opportunity in the first place. We can shrug off compliments, offset every positive with a blistering array of negatives, or endlessly compare ourselves to others by dramatically inflating them to be far more than what they really are so that we look far less than what we really are.

Proving Our Value

Or, we try to work against this despairingly negative sense of self by expending all of our energies to prove it wrong. Our lives devolve into these incessant tasks that never achieve their stated goal, leaving us convinced that despite our best efforts we are not worthy of our best efforts. Fundamentally, at the core of the desire to prove ourselves through achievement there are two fundamental needs. First is the need for identity. And second is the need for worth and value. If the basis of our identity and our sense of worth and value is rooted in achievement, (which is the stuff that we do), then we've always got to be doing. We've got no alternative except to always be on the run, always planning the next thing, always tediously mapping out the next endeavor to ensure that it's better than the last one, and always taking everything that we lay our hands on to the next level to the point that we eventually end up putting the next level entirely out of reach anyway.

Part of the perpetual frustration lies in the fact that the point at which we hope to gain this cherished sense of accomplishment to build ourselves or diminish ourselves is ill-defined. We have some vague and often wandering sense of it, or we've determined a general proximity of sorts. If it has sufficient clarity, we can be fairly certain that we've arrived. However, we're often doomed to realize that what we wanted this to do for us upon our arrival did not happen. Therefore, there's a sense that we failed on our way here, thereby robbing our arrival of what we hoped to gain from it. If our sense of it was unclear, we typically determine that we really have not arrived or we've arrived at the wrong place. Whether we are driven to prove ourselves worthy or unworthy, either way failure is certain.

Who or What's Driving Us?

William Frederick Book wrote that "A man must drive his energy, not be driven by it." We know that we expend energy, and typically we expend a lot of it. But we rarely question if we're driving our energy or if our energy is driving us. Who's in control here? We pound and we push and we perseverate and we plod along and when we get pummeled we pick ourselves up and press on. The relentless nature of it all rarely if ever gives us the time or the resolve to pull back, pause and ask who or what's controlling the energy that we're expending? And if we were to define success either in proving our worth or showing ourselves as worthless, defining what we're doing and why we're doing it would be a vitally important part of that process.

It would be reasonable to say that if we're not controlling the expenditure of our energy, if we're simply responding or reacting or being driven by something that we can't in reality achieve through whatever our efforts are, then the energy spent is wasted. The deceptive nature of it all is that just because we're expending energy we assume that something's being accomplished. The fact that we're doing so much could only result in some sort of goal attainment. Something good and successful (in whatever way we've defined success) must be coming out of this simply because the energy we're putting out has to be resulting in something . . . doesn't it?

Productivity as Value
Productivity is often defined by expenditure, even though the two may not correlate at all. We're busy about being busy, and somehow being busy suggests purpose. We're pounding out this thing that we call life, as if the pounding has a purpose other than the pounding. We're fighting the battles, climbing the mountains, forging though whatever wilderness we think we're in, and charting out journeys of glorious adventure. We're pressing through the obligations of the day and the challenges of the week. Or, we're

working hard to believe that we're not worth believing in so that we can finally lay ourselves to rest because we have no value to lay our lives upon. Either way, we're busy and we believe that our busyness evidences our value.

Our value, however, is not believed to be a constant. Therefore, to maintain our value we have to remain busy. Yet beyond that, there is some glitch in the human psyche that says that to have consistent value, we have to be consistently busier. That what worked today will be inadequate tomorrow. That what was sufficient this week will be woefully insufficient next week. That proving one's worth through busyness requires a perpetual escalation of busyness to the point that there are simply not enough hours in a single day or a collection of days to be that busy. We will fail. But we will view ourselves as the failure rather than understanding the sheer impossibility of the dynamic.

The Privilege of a Place
However, the things that we do, despite the positive or negative nature of them, illustrate the fact that life has crafted a place for us and therefore we have a purpose. Life has deemed us of sufficient value to carve out a spot that is uniquely ours. We have the privilege of having been gifted with this life and having been handed the authority to live it in out in whatever way we choose to live it out. In fact, we

have been tasked with living it in a way that is entirely unique to us. We have been granted a privilege unlike anyone we will ever meet.

We might be using that privilege negatively. We might be using it to our own demise. We might be turning it against ourselves. But we have the privilege of having a place that is uniquely ours, regardless of what we choose to do with it. And because we have all of these things that life has granted us and subsequently called us to do, we obviously must have value. We have been granted the privilege of both life and choice because we have sufficient value to have been granted those privileges in the first place. We might misuse them, but we have them to misuse. And that means that we were good enough to be granted them in the first place.

What Drives Us Drives Our Energy

It's the fact that we've been called. We have a purpose that is uniquely ours. We've been granted a niche. We have a place at the table. We have a place that has been specifically reserved in this eons-long thing that we call life. Yes, deep down we want to be successful. As we have said, the reality that we have been granted this place in life evidences the fact that we are of sufficient worth to be there regardless of success or lack thereof.

However, having been granted this place does not appear sufficient for us to feel that we have real worth and substantive value. Our low self-esteem lulls us into believing that we don't actually belong here...at all. It speaks to us in tones either loud and deafening or quiet and bedeviling that this is not our place. Therefore, we have to prove that we are worthy to be here. We have to show that this calling or these privileges weren't a fluke, or something that we fabricated out of our desperation to feel that we have value. We have to make this real. We can't simply bow in grateful appreciation for what life has bestowed upon us. Rather, we have to prove that we are worth the bestowing.

Because we have embraced this line of thinking, our energies are expended on our attempts at achieving something in order to prove our worth in the place that we've been granted. We've got to achieve, for if we don't maybe we weren't good enough for this place in the first place. We've got to earn our place. But while we're expending energy holding our place through the earning of that place, we have to earn our way to the next place at the very same time. We have this sense that the place we're at has limited value. That in the ever-incessant flow of life, wherever we're at has a really short shelf life. We know that soon it will become the place that we should have left in pursuit of the place that we should be going. The accolades of today's achievement can quickly become the murmuring of tomorrow's questions as people begin to wonder why we're still sitting in yesterday.

Therefore, we fight to stay where we're at while simultaneously fighting to move into tomorrow. We desperately want to solidify our current position, but not so much that we inadvertently lock ourselves into it. We must lay rigorous claim to the moment in order to preserve it as the step to the next moment, for if the former fails that latter will never exist to be given a chance to fail.

It Doesn't Work – Wasted Energy

With that all said, whether we actually achieve what we're out to achieve or not (whether that be good or bad), in reality it neither defines us nor establishes our worth. Whether we rise to some position of prominence, or achieve some step, or have a litany of letters stacked up behind our name or cross some ill-defined finish line, none of these have any bearing on our worth or value. Our energies have all been about the achievement of whatever goals we've set for ourselves as a means of evidencing the fact that we are worth a place at the table. And while all of the trappings of doing all of this stuff appears to build us up, the trappings are in fact the very trap that will leave us living out our lives surrounded by successes, but engulfed in the forever question of "Am I good enough?"

The need to achieve these goals controls our energy, not us. We have this terribly rampant fear of not knowing who we are and subsequently having

41

absolutely no grounding at all to effectively engage life as it roars at us, spins around us, and challenges us to do something with it and about it. Or, we have this terribly desperate feeling that our worthlessness has become completely exposed due to the fact that we stand here with nothing to hold up to show that we have value, and that based on our inability to evidence our value we have no inherent right to the place we've been granted. Therefore, we stand shamed before the whole world. Or, we do the opposite and we sabotage our situation to prove that we don't belong here rather than working to prove that we do (which isn't any more helpful).

And then we start asking ourselves a host of terrifying questions. What if none of this works? What if we don't measure up? What if we fail life? What if we look the part but are nothing of the part? What if it was all energy spent and wasted in the spending? What if we were the fool and we just postponed the reveal? Living with ourselves in a manner such as this is dying dressed in the façade of living.

Easing the Panic
And so we default to achievement to rectify it all and get rid of the questions. If we achieve, it all goes away. If we achieve we can hold up the mirror of whatever we've achieved, point to it and say, "See, that's me, that's who I am, and therefore I do belong in the place life afforded me." We can grab that

mirror and gaze into it every time our self-esteem wanes or teeters on some precarious edge. We can carry it around with us and peer into it when this perpetually flagging sense of self starts to flag. We can do this until the mirror doesn't work anymore and we begin to fall into the trap of believing that maybe we don't belong here.

Achievement says we have value because we can point to the validation of the achievement, that we took nothing and made something from it which says that we do have a place and a purpose. That we stood in the face of both searing criticism and daunting obstacles, and in the standing we bested them both. That we overcame. We won.

But in reality, these things neither define who we are or substantiate our value. Our energies are horribly misdirected and tragically wasted because those precious energies are entirely controlled and completely disseminated by these convincing illusions that are destined to fade and die. We can't prove our worth and value through achievement of any sort. And until we recognize this, we will live our lives very much 'out-of-sorts.'

However, rather than understanding that these never work despite the best of our energies, we fall into the trap and we assume that 'we' didn't make them work. We presume that we just weren't good enough. We determined that we didn't have the wherewithal and that we lacked enough of everything that was needed to become something. It just wasn't in us. Subsequently, we mentally and emotionally bury ourselves in a place that we never should have been in in the first place.

Our Value as Internal, Not External

Despite the screaming message of the culture and the declarations of those on lesser ventures, our value rests in who we are, not in what we do with who we are. Without a doubt, what we do with who we are has value, but it does not grant us value because that value already existed prior to any achievement. Our existence alone is the greatest statement of our worth and the clearest evidence as to our value. What we do with that existence is up to us. But the sheer reality of that existence evidences value. The fact I am writing this and you are reading this attests to the fact that we both have immense value because we both exist to do those things.

Have you considered the fact that without who we are, what we do would not exist? Every victory, every achievement, every accomplishment hinges on the fact that we were there to do it. Therefore, what we do is entirely dependent upon our existence. All that we do emerges from everything that we are: our gifts, our talents, our abilities, our qualities, our characteristics, our attributes and so on. What we do is simply a manifestation of all of those things expressing themselves in whatever we've put our mind to expressing them.

Deserving Our Place at the Table

That is why we were granted the place of privilege that we were granted. That is why we have a seat at the table. What we do is simply a manifestation of who we are working itself out into what God already knows us to be. We would be much better served to use our energies to bring growth and maturation to who we are, not to squander those energies in our attempts to prove who we are or establish who we are not. This is not to say that achievement is bad. In reality, achievement is very good and we are privileged to attain it. Rather, it's to say that achievement for the wrong reasons or misplaced motivations is damaging.

We don't have to prove that we are worthy of the places that life has granted us. Yes, we need to be thankful for them. We need to cherish them. We need to hold them in high regard and never minimize them. But we've been given them because we've been deemed equipped for them. There's nothing to prove. What's the sense in attempting to prove what's already been proven? There's just the work that we've been blessed to do and the positions we've been blessed to have. And those are not granted to us to prove anything to anybody. Rather they are given to us to bless and maximize everything.

Mentally that's a tough shift to make. It's a reversal of epic proportions and the fact that it is evidences the depth of the lie that we've been living. Each of us needs to embrace the fact that our value is in who we are. And we need to widen that thought by understanding that this value that we carry within us exceeds our greatest estimation of it. It will readily eclipse anything that we do. That value is already there within us, even if we don't see the far-reaching nature of it. Seeing something is not necessary to evidence its existence. It rests in exercising the faith that to be human is to possess potential. To be a child of God is to possess the infinite. And to possess infinite potential means that there's a grand mission for the manifestation of it. Therefore we don't need to create something or prove that potential. We only need to rest in it and let everything flow from it.

The Hard Questions:
1. If I look at all of the things that I do, what is it that I have within me that has allowed and/or equipped me to do those things ?
2. Once I've identified those things, what would happen if they were all taken from me?
3. What then does this say about what is truly valuable about me?

Craig D. Lounsbrough

Chapter Four
The Shaping of Me
Who I Am and Who I'm Not

"Before I formed you in the womb I knew you, before you were born I set you apart; I appointed you as prophet to the nations."
-   Jeremiah 1:5 (NIV)

"You cannot dream yourself into a character; you must hammer and forge yourself one."
-   Henry David Thoreau

"Who Am I?" What the Question Evidences

"Who am I?" The question seems a bit overused these days. It's something more like a vogue, trendy kind of question that pulls us out of the doldrums of living among the masses and plants us in the more desirable currents of the intellectual mainstream. In our culture, I tend to think it's less about thoughtfully unearthing who we are as a means of living in awe of what God wrought within us. Rather, I think it's more about creating something that's culturally acceptable and that adheres to the contrivances of whatever trend is currently trending in the culture. It's the creation of a self-suitable to the world rather than discovering who we are as both in and above the world.

The question of 'who we are' suggests that we're exercising our intellectual acumen to probe our existence. That exercise itself lends weight to the fact that we have an intellect to exercise and an existence to live it out in. By its very nature the question of 'who we are' poses the thesis that we are something other than being nothing, and that 'something' has relevance when 'nothing' doesn't. By asking the question we reveal the need that we possess to believe that we exist and that our existence is purposeful. We want to believe that we are supposed to become 'something' rather than float around being 'nothing' going nowhere. To ask the question is to evidence the fact that we are beings in need of asking the question. And that in and of itself evidences the incredible depth and unparalleled richness of our humanity.

In addition, the question of 'who we are' also suggests that a simple answer is simply not suitable. That some cheesy pabulum will not suffice. That the definitions proposed by innumerable philosophers and those who for centuries have probed the inner workings of life aren't quite enough. That holding ourselves up against everyone else in order to grasp some sense of who we are by comparing ourselves to who everyone else is simply repeatedly comes up short. That aligning with political hashtags or running off after a litany of causes that have caught the wandering eye of those without a cause doesn't answer the question. That even though we've gorged ourselves on self-help philosophies and immersed ourselves in the rigors of mindfulness (or any one of the many other popular contrivances) we still don't have the answer.

And that is not necessarily that all of these things are incorrect or that they don't speak something of truth into our lives. It's not that at some level they don't have some sort of value. It's that they're not enough. The cumulative weight of their collected insights falls short. Mankind has asked the question of "Who am I"? for as long has mankind has existed. And yet in the end, we don't have an answer that explains the whole of who we are. After untold millennia we are still on this search and we are still asking this question.

And if all of this evidences anything at all, it evidences the depth of our depth. It speaks to the innate and persistent complexity of who we are. Stored within the body, mind and soul of each of us there is a vastness that all of the combined explorations of mankind have yet to fathom, much less understand. And can we not correlate this complexity and depth with our value? Everything in existence has value for the place that it holds in relationship to everything else. But we stand apart in complexity, intellect, reasoning and ability. We have been equipped for and tasked with the responsibility to care for everything else and nothing else has been assigned that role...except us. Indeed, does this not evidence our value?

How Do We Not Know?

The ever-baffling fact regarding the question of 'who we are' is that we live with 'us' every single solitary day of our existence. Yet, even though we live with 'us' with a transparent intimacy that no one else in all of existence ever will, we still don't know 'us.' How could that be? How could we wake up every day and go to bed every night with this person that we are and still not know who we are? How is it that we walk through the myriad array of dynamics and demands of life and living, and somehow do not see ourselves in the act of dealing with those things? How have we lived with ourselves yet missed ourselves in the living? Yes, as we have stated, we are phenomenally complex. However, is there something else?

We Don't Want to See

One answer is that we don't want to see. We don't want to see because we fear that if we actually look at who we are, we might not like who or what we see. It may confirm our deepest fears about who we are. It may affirm the presence of something we desperately hoped wasn't there, or it may confirm the absence of something that we hoped was. It may convince us that we really don't have the capacity to achieve the dreams that we want to achieve. It may corroborate all of the negative things that people have said we are, when we've spent our lives fighting against believing that that's who we are. We may choose 'ignorance' as opposed to 'knowing' so that

50

we can continue wearing the weathered façade that we've found comforting, in whatever way it might comfort us.

Or, looking at ourselves might actually confirm that we are better than what we thought ourselves to be, which will result in some sort of accountability that we don't want. It may highlight rather formidable parts of ourselves that we haven't cultivated, or personal resources that we've wasted in the wasting. It may reveal potential that has languished in the pit of ignorance, or giftings that have been left to rot in the sewers of apathy. It may call us up to places that we don't believe we can go, leaving us greatly vexed by the contradiction of it all. So, we don't want to see because seeing is just too painful, or too demanding, or too burdensome, or it comes weighted with too much guilt.

Becoming What They Want

Or, we've spent our energies not coming to understand who we are but on becoming whoever it is that everyone says we should become. There are demanding social pressures to adhere to. Heavy-handed societal expectations that press us for compliance. There are those who are committed to whatever politically correct agenda they're committed to who are easily aroused and readily enflamed to rage should we refuse alignment with their agendas. There are the voguish trends that demand adherence lest we be labeled as outdated or just plain ignorant. There are the expectations of parents that rest heavy upon us, and the voices of well-meaning mentors that too often called us to some vision of who they thought we were. Therefore, we don't have time to see ourselves because we're spending our time trying to become another 'self.'

Pressured to conformity by these elements, we develop this sectarian view of what we should be. We've collected this societal and relational collage that appears to be a perpetually changing montage of what we're supposed to be. Somehow this becomes the standard template in place of ourselves being that standard. Over time, we are lulled into believing that the pursuit of this template is the truest pursuit of self, when it is nothing of the kind. And we become what we are not.

Being What Circumstances Made Us
It's possible that we might have determined that it's not who we are, but who circumstances made us to be. Abuse as a child. Bullying at the hands of thoughtless people bent on propping up their own fragile insecurities at our expense. Jobs lost in acquisitions that sacrificed employees on the cold altar of budget and profit. Marriages that collapsed at the hands of spouses who decided that the trade-off between personal agendas and the life of a marriage and family was legitimate. Enemies that we mistook for friends who slowly circled around

behind us and stabbed us in one of the many ways that people stab others. For us, these answer the question, "Who am I?"

The wounds, the disappointments, the betrayals, and the losses both large and small have defined us. In addition, the process of healing from the wounds inflicted, as well as angst involved in waiting for the ones that are yet to happen, further defines who we are. The embracing of an existence defined by what happened to us, further shaped by what we fear will happen becomes the sum total of who we are. Our lives become a tragically circular story of being wounded and then healing only to be wounded yet again. The difficult issue in being defined by our circumstances is that to understand how all of that has defined us means that we have to think about how all of that has defined us. And in our mind, the pain of doing that far, far offsets any potential self-discoveries. So we don't think about them (or at least we try not to).

There's Nothing to Discover
Or, we don't feel that there's any identity to discover. That somehow we are the embodiment of a bunch of 'nothing' that will only add up to nothing. That because there's nothing there, the need for some sort of pursuit becomes unnecessary and embarrassingly ridiculous. We are what we already know, despite how little that might be. Somehow we ended up at the shallow end of the gene pool, or we showed up

late when things were being handed out. We got to rummage through the leftovers or we were looked over. There was no motivation to develop anything along the way, or the opportunities to do so simply never came our way. Therefore, we don't know who we are because we're pretty much nothing and we already know that.

From nothing you can only get nothing. So we become embedded in a sense of hopelessness regarding both the present that we live in and the future that we have come to dread. The journey of self doesn't exist because there's nothing to journey from, and nothing to journey to. There's a settling of sorts, where we fall into a sedentary malaise. And in this place where everything is nothing, our soul slowly stops breathing.

Other Reasons
Or could it be something entirely different? Could it be that we are vast beyond comprehension? That we've mistaken this journey of 'who am I' for a destination that gives us a clear and solid answer versus seeing it as a journey where the answer is always fleshing itself out with ever-great clarity as we go along? That we are perpetually in the process of becoming more of whoever we are? That we are not meant to be something that's stagnant in time and space, but rather something that is always evolving in a manner such that we are constantly advancing into time and growing in space? And to

understand that is to begin to build a sense of self that will effectively begin to disassemble our negative self-esteem.

All of this implies that we are, in fact, created vast beyond comprehension. And this personal vastness is so vast that it gifts us with resources that are beyond the years that we have to live out those resources. We are bigger than our own lifespan. Therefore, 'who we are' is based on 'who we are in the becoming of who we are.' Who we are is not defined by some sedentary event such as an alliance, or someone's expectations of us, or the events that have befallen us. And unless we understand that, we will have missed the process of becoming who we are by looking for an answer in all the other things that can't answer the question.

The Size of 'Who I Am'
We have been gifted with a depth that will invite exploration and make space for such exploration for the entirety of our lives. We will never discover something about ourselves that will be that distinctly final discovery that concludes the journey. New vistas, fresh insights, and breathtakingly vast levels of awareness always await. We are entirely fluid, having each thing we learn expand upon everything that we learned before it, and subsequently enhancing everything that we've yet to learn. We grow geometrically, moving out in every direction at every moment in a continual cascade of

expansion. The end of who we are exists only as a figment of our sorely limited imaginations and is an outcome of the fear that maybe we are more than we've allowed ourselves to be.

What we do know is that we are the sum total of what we know about ourselves, plus the infinitely larger part that we don't know. There will never be the final question. That every answer to every question is an invitation to the next question and the next one after that. We are people made of horizons and for horizons, and if perchance we live within walls, it is we who have created them. The question of "Who am I?" is not one question answered by one answer. It is a robust collection of questions that slowly but deliberately reveal the tantalizing picture of who we are. It is an adventure of the greatest sort. The hunt for treasure that captivates all of our imaginations. It is discovering the genius of God as that genius is manifest within us without any hesitation of any kind. Hence the question, "Who am I?"

This search itself blatantly evidences the fact that we are bigger than ourselves, for if we knew everything about ourselves a search would be unnecessary and the questions unprovoked. There is more to us than we know, and even though we live in union with ourselves every day we remain a mystery to ourselves. Despite our low self-esteem and incessant deprecation, the question of who we are evidences that there is more to us than we realize.

And if we walk out this search for self, at some inherently deep level we know that 'who we are' is so vast that we will spend the entirety of our lives in search of it, yet we will never know all of it. And if the whole of us is beyond the whole of a lifetime to discover, how indescribably grand must we be? Maybe this is what should shape our self-esteem. This is how we should view ourselves. This is what fires our imagination and fuels our journey.

Seeking the Answer Versus Searching for Peace

The question then begs the search, which can be unsettling for many. The penetrating angst and unrelenting curiosity generated by the question of 'who we are' is the impetus that sends us searching for some sense of peace about who we are. This peace is not necessarily obtained by having some answer to the question. The frenzied search to calm our souls often sends us into the 'plug-and-play' of a culture ready to give us the once-over and then plug us into whatever the once-over has determined us to be. It becomes something of a search for the defining box that our careers hand us, or the identifying label that our social circles have crafted for us, or the place that our socio-economic status defines as ours, or the role that our family or friends have etched out for us.

The Self That I Long to Believe In

There's a myriad army of people and philosophies and social structures ready to dress us up and deck us out in the borrowed garments woven of their biases and stitched tight by their sordid agendas. Should it have its way, the world would abscond with us, embezzling our resources in the service of its agendas. And while all of these might give us an identity, that identity is borrowed or imposed or both. Suffice it to say, an identity either borrowed or imposed is a costume parading itself around as something it is not. At best, it may grant us a fragile and fraudulent peace that we gladly mistake for the real thing.

However, it lacks sustenance and stability. Typically, it's constructed to fit a space suited for those who created it, rather than knock down the walls that have constricted us. It's what fits them, but what enslaves us. Therefore, we have to repeatedly adjust it as we might, tear it down when we tire of it, build it back up when we're scolded for tearing it down, and repeat the worn out narrative of why this is us and why it works...when it's not and it doesn't. Subsequently, the question goes unanswered because we don't have the time to ask it.

Because it doesn't work, our low self-esteem sits on forlorn hands and tells itself that the search is impossibly complex and that we would wise to relegate ourselves to some static existence of some sort. We are either nothing, or we are something that we are not, or we are all things bad built upon all things bad. We end up in one of these places because we've come at this defining question from every possible angle except the right one.

Within Not Without

As patently simplistic as it sounds, we are defined by who we are. We need not reach out to everything around us in order to define that which is within us. If we reach out to something or someone outside of us in this search for self, whatever or whoever we reach out to needs to walk us back inside of us because that's where we are. It's about being intelligently introspective in a manner that is intentional, thoughtful and relentless. It is about peeling away the sticky layers of culturally imposed norms, digging through the impregnable strata of our histories, breaking out of all of the superimposed roles, and rigorously erasing all of the rogue messages that others have penned across the tablet of our souls. And in the upheaval of a process that grand, it's then formulating the right questions hoping that we're actually daring enough to ask them.

In this rigorous process, it's not about evaluating what we see as held against some clandestine societal rubric or chafing personal bias. Rather, it's more about accepting what we see and asking how it can be shaped, honed, cultivated and nurtured. It's about believing that we were created with all the essential elements to become the person that we were intentionally and rather ingeniously designed to be. It's about understanding that there is a specific role out there somewhere that's waiting for us to show up and that it's probably sitting a whole lot closer to us than we think it is. And the best way that we can show up for that role is to come as we are and not as the world says we should come. It's presenting ourselves before the God that created us, stepping into the life He set in front of us, and believing that it will unfold if we just show up for everything to unfold.

This is not about giving ourselves permission to spin off on some ill-defined quest of self-indulgence, for our true selves won't find themselves shaped for that kind of agenda. This is not about permission to become absorbed in a self-satiating endeavor where we suddenly realize that life is ours for the taking when we've spent our lives having life take from us. Rather, it's respecting our authenticity as being something that adds to life rather than adds to self. It's about realizing that our true self will never detract from the true selves of those around us nor will it ever impinge upon them. And if perchance it does, it wasn't 'us' to begin with.

You are uniquely designed with everything you need to be everything that you are. And that design is sufficient to be able to do everything that you were designed to do. It is big enough to exceed your lifetime. You may not see it, but as have noted, seeing something does not evidence its existence or lack thereof. It's coming against the lies that have been spun about us, the identities that have been forced upon us, and breaking the box that other, more fearful people have crafted for us. Despite the nature of your self-esteem and the darkness that it has layered 'round about you, may the quest to discover all of this be relentless in its scope, potent in its process and blessed throughout.

The Hard Questions:

1. If you were to die, what one accomplishment would give you a sense that your life was meaningful?

2. What would be the core trait or primary characteristic of the thing that you've chosen?

3. In what way could you manifest that core trait throughout your life?

Chapter Five
Bigger on the Inside Than the Outside
Attempting to Define Success to Define Ourselves

"Very truly I tell you, whoever believes in me will do the works I have been doing, and they will do even greater things than these, because I am going to the Father."
- John 14:12 (NIV)

"Continuous effort – not strength or intelligence – is the key to unlocking our potential."
- Winston Churchill

Success has been accorded an endless array of definitions. Some of them are crafted to make failure seem more like success so that we can limp through life and fail without remorse or guilt. Other definitions are quite lofty, written to give us opportunity to achieve in a manner that has little to do with the achievement and everything to do with restoring blunted self-esteems. At times success is defined by whatever will accord us the accolades of others or advance us socially or professionally. At yet other times, the definition of success is more about giving ourselves a sorely needed boost when our spirits have been lagging.

Sometimes definitions are crafted as we go along, granting us permission to fluidly and rather nonchalantly alter the definition of success in order to form-fit whatever the outcome of our choices have been. In doing that, we have granted ourselves full license to define the outcome in whatever way suits our choices. We can craft a definition of success to embolden a faltering cause or create support when our base is splintering and our people are wavering.

Then there are other times when the definition of success is modified to diminish the works of those we've come to abhor and elevate those upon whom our favor has fallen. Some definitions of success are those shaped by the shifting pen of political correctness, or the placating tenets of the culture, or the gnawing need for acceptance, or the dictates of a particular social grouping that demands adherence to a prescribed set of standards. Sometimes success is defined by the proclamations of some revered leader, or the family system that we grew up in, or the job description that shapes our nine-to-five lives.

Lost in the Array of Definitions

Whatever and wherever their source, a dizzying array of definitions abound. Many seem to be a target created after the trigger was pulled, making every decision a bullseye even if the aim was horrid. Some are thrown out because they're easy, or we're not certain what success is so we just come up with something that might pass for success if people don't pay too much attention. And in the squalor of definitions gone awry and rogue, we seem to have lost a genuine definition of success.

Subsequently, it is this mad array of definitions that sends us scurrying in a million different directions in order to be successful in whatever way success is defined at the moment. We might not know what success is, but if we do well enough in enough areas, or if we adhere to enough of the things defined as trendy and vogue, or if we chase whatever everyone else is chasing we just might happen to land on something successful. Maybe it's the proverbial 'shot in the dark' that might altogether miss, yet the fact that we took the shot itself was defined as success regardless of what it hit. In the end, success becomes more defined by figuring out exactly what success is rather than actually fulfilling the definition.

Why Success?
It's interesting that success, in whatever manner it is defined, has come to define our worth and value. That's why a lack of perceived success will tank our self-esteem quicker than just about anything else. Success appears to have become the litmus test as to the credibility of our existence and the unforgiving gauge of our worth. Success has evolved into the exclusive commodity by which we ascribe value to ourselves and others. It's the thing that gives us status, grants us credibility, authenticates what we say, lends weight to our opinions, and awards us

with the sense of a life well lived. It is the crown jewel of our existence, something to be vigorously pursued and rigorously obtained at all costs, for not doing so is a life squandered, opportunity lost and self-esteem decimated. We are led to believe that to not be successful is to live out the story of this sorry existence of ours without having validated the legitimacy of the existence that we wasted.

Fear of Questioning the Definition

Success becomes so acutely defined and so irrevocably defining that we seldom entertain any other possible definition. We find ourselves entangled in the culturally mandated definition of success, or the definitions imposed by our families or friends or occupation. We become so absorbed in the sorting out and the achieving of those definitions that the endeavor to achieve them becomes inordinately consuming. We have little tolerance to question the definition of success because we were told that we shouldn't...so we don't. Or, the pursuit of it is so intense that we never stop long enough to question it. And if we did, we fear that the cultural definition might be incorrect or our families would get sufficiently perturbed that our lives will have forever run amuck because we missed the cherished mark in the questioning of it. So we don't question it.

Therefore, given that the defining scale of success has assumed such a dominant role in our culture, and given that we presume there to be some golden definition out there, we must find a definition for it or at least write one that would be approved of. Otherwise we have no precise framework by which to determine our success or lack thereof. Once we feel we've landed on the singular definition of success, we throw ourselves into the chase for fear that our lives might devolve into obscurity, our legacy might be pathetic, and we ourselves remain contemptible. But what does this mean in terms of how we've come to identify who we are and in that, how we've attempted to determine the value of who we are?

What We Do or Who We Are?

As we have noted in a previous chapter, too often the yardstick that we use to measure our worth is defined by 'what we do.' What we do is measured by a series of accomplishments, the manner in which we have embellished life through those accomplishments, and the achievement of goals lofty behind the imagination of the common man and far beyond the reach of the hoards. It's understanding what's fundamentally achievable and then embracing the belief that our worth is defined as raising oneself significantly above that which is fundamentally achievable. It's being intentional about ascending to some lofty escarpment that we ourselves had deemed impossible to surmount. Therefore, the definition of success is the measurement of accomplishment.

In applying this standard, we evidence our worth as held up against the enormity of the task itself and the manner in which the everyday person accomplishes the task. If we can eclipse both, we feel that we have established our worth by virtue of these comparisons. But eclipsing both requires determining what success is so that we know we achieved it. 'What we do' is granted credibility by whatever our definition of success is. Without the definition, we have nothing by which to measure 'what we do.' We won't know if we hit it or not. And in our minds, if that definition hasn't been met or if the bullseye hasn't been hit, everything that we do becomes the everything that achieves nothing.

The Flaw of Success
Yet, the nature of such a mentality of success demands that we constantly achieve. It is an effort of insanely perpetual works that requires that we continually prove our worth as the previous success eventually fades sufficiently to demand a new one. Sure, we can define it. But success as used to determine our worth and value is always temporal. It's always moving. Therefore, we become enslaved to successes that demand nothing more than other successes. It becomes apparent that success is a temporary aphrodisiac that will always demand more of itself without helping us develop any sense of worth regarding ourselves. Understanding this, success then might be best defined as breaking the

need to be successful as a means of proving our value.

We have to break this need to be successful because success becomes a morbid cycle where we become successfully defeated. As noted, success in and of itself is not a problem nor is it bad unless it becomes the standard by which we measure our worth and value. Success that evidences our worth must be repeated without an end because there is no success great enough to grant us a sustained sense of worth and value. We are worth far more than any success might impute. Because that's the case, success must be revisited again and again because it can speak little into something as vast as we are.

We Are Too Big to Be Defined By Any Success
As we noted in a previous chapter, our value is not based on 'what we do.' Rather, it is based on 'who we are.' If we remain stuck with the feeling that our worth is based on 'what we do,' the definition of success is what lends credence to those efforts. The definition of success gives 'what we do' a mark to shoot for and a distinct line to cross. It lends clarity to where we're going and when we get there. Yet, we can hit the mark and cross the line and raise our arms in ardent celebration with our self-esteem none the better for the experience.

Success is irrelevant in respect to our self-esteem as any definition of success regardless of how lofty does not possess the power to sustain our sense of worth or feed our sense of value. When it comes to our sense of worth and value, success is the thing that's not the thing. It's been marketed as the snake oil for our self-esteem by the carpetbaggers of our culture, but it's snake oil only. The quietly alluring aspect of success is that it promises a perpetual sustenance and feeding of our self-esteem. It whispers the message in a rather seductive and convincing manner. Given that the culture has fallen for its smooth talk and has subsequently run pell-mell after its message, its legitimacy is reinforced.

However, it is always in need of resuscitation. Success cannot do what it promises to do. It cannot deliver on time. It comes with wild promises but empty hands. It spouts great platitudes that thrill the listener, but it crashes with such force that it shatters the eardrums. With such an apparently irreconcilable flaw in its makeup, it would be worthwhile to postulate that our worth must be based on something significantly more consistent and profoundly more fundamental than success.

We Want to Define What Defines Us

The great rub that keeps us from getting out of this rut is that we want to define what defines us. We can acknowledge that the definition of success does not grant us worth and value. We can understand that, believe that, and come to accept that. We've chased these imposed definitions long enough to know that the chasing never resulted in the catching. But instead of understanding that our value is not based on any definition of success, we determine that the definition is wrong and that we can right that.

When the promise of those definitions begin to falter, we spend our time covertly crafting alternative definitions. Since this other route has failed us, we can craft life, impose the values, shift the circumstances and modify a host of other variables that eventually shape a fresh definition of success in order to give us a maximum chance of success.

The failure of all this lies in the fact that we did not learn from the failure that we just experienced. We're repeating the very thing that we said we're no longer doing. We didn't learn that it can't be done. We just thought that it couldn't be done the way that society did it or our families did it, so we tried to do it differently. We missed the fundamental lesson that our value is not based on what we do as defined by the definition of success, regardless of who creates the definition or how appealing it might be. We lived the lesson, but we missed the very thing that we were living. We missed the lesson that maybe success is believing that we already are a success by virtue of our existence and that our calling is not to prove it, but

70

to act upon it.

It's the pursuit of success and the failure of what it promises that leads us to errantly believe that we are not successful. That we have failed being successful, or that we were not successful enough. That maybe we were deluded into thinking that we were successful when we weren't and we just didn't know it. That in some capacity and in some manner that we've yet to identify, we failed even though we honestly thought that we didn't. In fact, we didn't fail. Rather, success failed us because it cannot deliver what it promises. So, there must be another avenue.

Value Based on Who We Are
As we noted previously, maybe we should dare to consider that our worth does not need to be established either by effort or definition. Maybe we should consider the possibility that it has never not been established. That success was achieved by the fact that God decided to design us and then deliver us into a far larger design to make an impact in and upon that design. We're here, and that itself is a success.

Everything that we do from here forward is not about success, for success has already been achieved by the fact of our existence. It's about calling. It's about fulfillment of the purpose that we've been given the privilege to fulfill. It's about homing in on our purpose and purposefully carrying it out. It's about obedience to the call, not the adherence to some definition that measures our obedience. It's doing all of that knowing that our worth and value exists by virtue of the fact that we exist. From there on out, it's about the doing and not about the proving.

If this is the case, then the attempt to establish something that is already established is about attempting to prove something that is already true and has always been so. And if that is true, it doesn't need us to establish its value. The need is for us to believe it. To work it out in our attitudes and live it out in our lives. To rest in it and on it even at those moments when we don't feel it. To speak it into our existence when the world would speak something entirely different into our existence. And that rests squarely upon us.

Thinking a Bit More Deeply
It would therefore be wise to consider the possibility that our worth is based on something so profound and unerringly rich that its worth singularly speaks for itself. Something that does not need to be proven simply because it is established in a manner that the need of proof is the weakness of our vision and not the fact of reality. It would make sense that our worth should be, and in reality is, based on something that cannot be proven for any other reason than its value lies forever beyond the most

magnificent achievements that would serve to even remotely evidence it.

Could It Be That We Are More?
Could it be that we are more than we are? That we have a limit that has no limits? That in fact, we are not destined for limits, and that any that we have are those that we have taken upon ourselves? Are we set apart from the rest of our existence because we are not bound to that existence? We are forever pressing against the boundaries because we assume that something exists beyond them and that something exists within us to take us beyond them. We have this sense that our limits are nothing more than opportunities to expose these limits as the next step to the next place. We are always pressing ourselves outside of ourselves. The life truly lived is the life that is always calling itself outside of itself. Therefore, at what point do we reach this impenetrable wall that defines the end of whatever it is that we are? The answer is, we don't. And we might ask why we don't.

I would propose that next to God Himself, the thing of single greatest value is ourselves. The priceless nature of a single human life, despite the manner in which we've blithely degraded that worth, is wholly immense. And this immensity is utterly inestimable on so many indescribable levels that proof stands as entirely irrelevant.

Human beings stand as the most definitive accomplishment of creation, positioned as the pinnacle of a creation that is indescribably marvelous in and of itself. We are the final touch of the cosmos themselves. We are the defining brush stroke of a creation that encompassed the galaxies, raised up mountains, gouged out canyons, threw birds into flight, painted fiery sunsets and spun the mesmerizing diversity of the seasons. We are the thing for which these were created and we are the things that have been vested with the most improbable but most privileged job of caring for them.

We are God's defining work. There can be no shade of arrogance or darkening of pride in such a reality as that would only serve to sadly mar us and leave us with a diminished countenance. Indeed, we should be inordinately humbled that we are God's crowning achievement and that alone grants us inestimable worth. It is not about proving our worth through the sweaty efforts of success or achieving some definition thereof. It is about realizing successes of even the loftiest sort and boldest character could not in and of themselves prove our worth, for our worth is entirely inherent, undeniably priceless, and established in the fabric of creation itself.

Achieving for Sheer Pleasure, Not Proof of Value

74

We would be wise to embrace the liberating reality that we can achieve in life for the sheer pleasure of achievement, rather than as a despairing effort to establish our worth. We can walk through life with vigor and tenacity out of a sense of worth, not out of some desperate effort to prove our worth. We change things and we change the course of things because we have been privileged to possess both the ability and the permission to do so. Life is engaged, energized and inspired by our worth, rather than depleted in the pursuit of it. Our days are lived embracing the reality that our value is based on who we are, and to embrace that liberating reality is to embrace a life liberated.

The Viciousness of Low Self-Esteem Explained

In light of this, low self-esteem is the antithesis of who we are. It is ourselves fully removed from ourselves. It is the ultimate scorched-earth mentality that leaves the massiveness of who we are engulfed in smoke and razed in ashes. Of course low self-esteem is brutal. It must be if it is to have any impact upon the immensity of who we are. We are a vigorous lot, despite our frequent ignorance regarding that fact. Therefore, a low self-esteem must be relentless lest we shake it and reclaim our authentic selves in the shaking. Our enemy is formidable. But our resources are more formidable yet. Self-esteem would tell us that this is not true out of the fear that we might discover that it is and therefore bring the full weight of ourselves against it. You are what you don't see. You will always be what you don't see even if you choose to never see it. This is who you are and this is what you are.

If we cannot embrace this indisputable reality, we will be irreversibly stunted by the limitations of the achievements we pursue. We will chain our potential to the baseness of achievements. When we do, the infinite worth that defines us will be forever overshadowed by the shallowness of achievements, for the greatest achievements will never come close to reflecting our true value. Your value is based on who you are, despite what you do. And that is a critical but glorious shift that we each must make.

The Hard Questions:
1. What specific definition(s) of success have you come to embrace?
2. Why do you think that you've chosen to embrace these particular definitions?
3. If these are achieved, in what way do you feel they will have enhanced your sense of worth and value? For how long?

Chapter Six
Purpose
Do I Have One?

"'For I know the plans I have for you,' declares the LORD, 'plans to prosper you and not to harm you, plans to give you hope and a future.'"
- Jeremiah 29:11 (NIV)

"Learn to get in touch with the silence within yourself and know that everything in life has purpose. There are no mistakes, no coincidences, all events are blessings given to us to learn from."
- Elisabeth Kubler-Ross

We all throw around the idea of having a purpose, or not having one, or wondering if we're supposed to have one, or whatever we're wondering. We wonder if we really need a purpose, and if so do we create it or does it already exist and we just haven't happened to happen upon it just yet. For some of us, we think that the whole idea of having a purpose suggests that life is much more intentional than maybe we thought it was, and that maybe we're all part of a grand design of some sort.

For others of us who tend to see life as more happenstance, it's more about realizing how we can figure ourselves in to whatever's being figured out around us. In that sense, we create a purpose if what's around us appears to make it worthwhile or possibly necessary to do so. However, or in whatever way we go about it, we all ponder this whole idea of having a purpose. For having a purpose gives us a desperate sense of purpose when our self-esteem would tell us that we serve none.

There's something about life that doesn't quite make sense without a purpose. There's too much rhythm to life. There's too much that seamlessly meshes, even when scrutiny of the most exacting kind would not be able to ascertain how it possibly could. There's a beautiful and even mysterious connectivity that creates a dynamic unifying function, drawing everything together in some jointly corporate effort as a means of keeping everything moving and growing and flourishing. Even the darker side of life, perpetually roiling with its chaos and anarchy has an underlying cadence that maintains the darkness and feeds the destruction. Things have a place and a purpose in that place.

We Need a Purpose
Whatever the nature of our orientation might be, it seems that we need a purpose. There's a lot of things that we talk about and discuss and debate and ponder and pontificate about in life. We analyze and scrutinize a whole bunch of stuff. And most of those discussions are really all about sizing all of that stuff up in order to determine if we want to engage or not. Do we want to invest in those things, or learn more

about them, or build some part of them into our lives? Or do we categorize them as wholly irrelevant, blithely toss them aside, and move on from them to whatever the next thing's going to be? Most of our discussions are a part of this bit of shopping that we're doing in order to determine to if we want to purchase the product or pass on it.

But when it comes to purpose, it's not about shopping. Shopping implies that we have a choice. It suggests that we're leisurely strolling the endless aisles of life working out those endless decisions of whether we want to purchase something or not purchase something. There's a sense that we can live with or without whatever it is that's crammed onto the shelves that flank us on our left and on our right. The majority of these things are bright and shiny accessories that simply complement what we already have or lend a bit of accent to what we already believe in. In the complementing and the accenting, they don't necessarily add to what we have nor do they detract from it. Most of them are appealing options designed to supplement something, not sturdy truths constructed to support something. We can take them or leave them without any major repercussions in the taking or the leaving. That's most of life.

But purpose doesn't appear to be a bright and shiny accessory. It's not designed to 'supplement' anything because everything else is designed to supplement it. In fact, it's not an item that we choose to select or not select. Purpose doesn't leave us with the luxury of deciding whether we'll choose it or whether we won't. It's inborn. It's how we make sense of our existence as it's played out within the rest of existence. We have meaning because there's a role that makes sense of our existence and that serves to complement everything else in existence. It's simply not optional for purpose to be an option.

If we're going to live with fullness, we have to be fully committed to seeking out and working out our purpose. Otherwise, we will exist with a gaping internal vacuum that will leave our lives ill-defined, or worse yet, undefined. And herein we often discover the source of our damaged, raw and bleeding self-esteem. We feel that we have no purpose and that can only mean that we have no value.

The Question Regarding Our Purpose
Therefore, the question regarding purpose is not "do we need one?" The question regarding purpose is far beyond any tangled debate as to whether one is necessary. We can engage in the rather diffuse and ever-shifting debate of whether we have a purpose. We can ponder the subject and bring it under the scrutiny of political leanings, emerging philosophies, wildly divergent doctrines, the voice of the important people in our lives or other such

assorted maladies. Regardless of the microscope under which we put it or the template that we force upon it, it's not a question to be asked. Rather, it is a reality to be embraced.

Debates such as these often arise from those who would view life as this perpetually shifting expression of whatever they feel moved to express at any given moment. In such scenarios purpose gives way to the randomness of those who demand randomness as a platform to indulge whatever they wish to indulge whenever their mood moves them. Or, it arises from those who tightly align the idea of 'purpose' with the belief in a Superior Being that orchestrated this existence and our place in it. Wanting to reject all such notions of a God in order to hold tight to the gospel of self-determination, they reject all such notions of a purpose (or at least a divine one). Arguments such as these can likewise arise from those believe there's a purpose but fear the magnitude of it. In their minds, to know it and to pursue it is to risk failing at it. So, it's better not to know.

In reality, the question of purpose is simple, direct, but inherently complicated. The question demands bravery. It rises on the belief that we have an utterly indispensable role to play in our own existence because it is not just our own existence. Fulfilling our purpose has an equally critical role to play in the existence of others. It is our part in this ever-unfolding corporate story that we have been granted an indispensable part in.

It is to understand that despite our own sense of unworthiness, we have been given a purpose. The fact that we have a purpose is not so shaky as to be dependent upon our belief as to whether we're sufficient enough to have one. Quite the opposite. The fact that we have been granted a purpose evidences that we were worthy to have one. But more than that, we were sufficiently competent to play a role whose impact would move far beyond the limits of ourselves.

The Power and Scope of Purpose

To have a purpose is to possess power. For any purpose never begins and ends in itself. It is never that constricted, for then any purpose would be something so anemic that its very existence could not be justified. It never is held to the parameters of the life within which we live. Our purpose always moves out, as it never consolidates itself as a means of always moving in upon itself. Engaging in our purpose and working that purpose out has an influence far beyond the scope of the purpose itself. It is highly influential. It is the thing that builds upon the purposes of those around us, vigorously enhancing communities, nations and the global experience itself. To have a purpose is to possess power. And if we have been granted power of this sort, our value cannot be understated.

In fact, to not ask the question of what our purpose is, is to relegate our lives to mediocrity of the basest sort. It is to question the rationale of our existence as not existing. It causes us to debate the essence of who we are and what we're supposed to do with who we are, which in fact questions everything that we are. We possess the power and the freedom to ask the question. And I believe that we've been granted that authority so that in the asking we might find the purpose. The question is, "What is my purpose?" The question is not, "Do I have one?"

It's embracing that question and insistently asking it until we have the answer squarely in our hands so that we can begin to live it out squarely in our lives. That action both defines and breaks open our existence in ways few other things do. And it most certainly validates the worth of our existence in ways powerful and profound.

What "Purpose" Tells Us:
First, We're More Than Just the Sum Total of Our Existence

The fact that we have a purpose evidences the fact that we are more than just the sum total of whoever it is that we are. A purpose says that we have a much larger role in this thing that we call life than just the living out of our individual lives. Life is bigger than any of us will ever be as an individual. Purpose tells us that we're specifically designed to engage every bit of that expanse. Purpose tells us that everything that's within us is designed to engage everything that's outside of us, and there's a whole lot out there. A purpose tells us that we are far more than just the sum total of our existence because we are called to do something in an existence that far exceeds us. A purpose tells us that we are more than just "us."

Second, There is Something Greater Than Us That We're Invited to Participate In

The fact that we have a purpose tells us that is 'something else' out there. It tells us that the horizons in life don't come anywhere close to ending at the end of our existence as the single, solitary human beings that all of us are. The nature of purpose is such that it will always be bigger than us and it always live beyond us. It grants us the opportunity of legacy. It extends our influence beyond our own death when we're no longer here to extend it. These unshakeable realities substantiate the fact that there's more out there than we can possibly imagine. Purpose not only invites us out to embrace the wonder of imagining all of that, but it extends us a priceless invitation to actually step out into it. Gratefully, a purpose tells us that we are not the end of all that there is. In fact, 'we' are barely the beginning, and that in and of itself is wildly exciting. A purpose says that the 'out there' is far, far greater than the 'in here.' And it invites us out to freely run in it, to exuberantly play in it, and to potently transform all of it in the running and the playing.

Third, We're a Piece of a Much Larger Puzzle That Would Be Incomplete Without Us

Our purpose tells us that this massive world out there, as huge as it is, is sorely incomplete without us. As big and as enormous and as complicated and as intricate as the world is, it remains less than completely complete without us. We have a purpose in this world that only we can complete. Large or small, complicated or simple, breathtaking or life-giving, regardless of what our purpose is, the world will be incomplete unless we fulfill it. That makes each and every one of us terribly important in ways that most of us never even consider, and few of us even remotely conceptualize. We are utterly irreplaceable which makes every one of us invaluable beyond any sort of monetary reckoning that we could hope to calculate. Everything that's out there will be less than everything that's out there if we forsake our purpose. And that fact makes us incredibly valuable.

Fourth, We Do Not Need to Surrender to the Mundane

Our purpose tells us that life is intentional. It is to live out something not in the frustration of random happenstance, but in something for which this life was purposely designed. It tells us that we have the power and the mission to vividly enhance life, rather than living in some terribly foreboding mindset while we sit on 'pins and needles' anxiously waiting to see how life is going to play itself out. There is a destination that has enough meaning and sufficient value to call us to the challenges that will certainly be part of fulfilling that purpose. That we are not here to aimlessly pass by and leaving nothing in the passing. To the contrary, our existence is designed to live on beyond our existence. To leave a bold legacy of generational impact. To fight against all that fights against us in order to create space and grant opportunity for all of the things that would wish to live within us to be expressed outside of us. And to do this for those that walk beside us as well as those who will come behind us.

Fifth, We Can Deny It
Could it be that the first and foremost purpose of 'purpose' is to convince us that we have one? Is it likely that our purpose can only be fully manifest in a manner utterly transformational when we are convinced that we have a purpose to manifest? Possibly the most brilliant way that 'purpose' can do that is by granting us permission to deny that we have one. However rigorous the nature of the argument might be against having a purpose, we bring it to bear in our defense and we passionately pound whatever podium we're pounding on in that defense. And any reasonable person would hold that if we're putting so much thought, energy and passion into a defense of this sort, there must be something there to defend against. Therefore, it is our own

arguments against having a purpose that substantiates our actually having one.

We Don't Have to Create a Purpose, We Only Have to Find It

Purpose is not something that we create, or have to create, or can create. To do what it does, it must be exceedingly greater than what we could ever create it to be. It's not something that we create because it eclipses our vision and it lays leagues beyond the scope of our creativity. If we've created something that we've defined as our 'purpose' and we're chasing after whatever that is, what we're chasing is probably a nice idea or some collection of ideas. But it's not our purpose.

Rather, purpose is something that we find. It's not about tediously constructing some sort of purpose out of the scattered pieces and errant parts of whatever we understand ourselves and our lives to be. It's not about rummaging around the confines of our existence looking for ideas or sitting and awaiting the arrival of one of those ever-elusive moments of inspiration. It's not about figuring out how we build it or where we get the parts from in order to build it. God's done that work already, and He's done it with absolute perfection. Neither is it about earning it, for it was always yours and it was never not yours. Your very existence inarguably speaks to the fact that you have one.

We just need to commit ourselves to finding it. Not earning it but finding it. Not piecing it together but discovering that it was never in pieces in the first place. Next to our search for God, seeking out our purpose is one of the most phenomenal adventures that we will ever have the privilege of undertaking. As we've noted, it's a treasure hunt of the greatest sort. It's an adventure that leaves all other adventures as largely adventure-less. It's seeking out the very thing that we were designed to do. It undergirds and gives meaning to everything else. It is the rationale for our existence laid out on the table and explained. And it's there to be found if we commit to the search.

We Were Made for Our Purpose

Once we begin to quit denying our purpose or quit attempting to manufacture it, the nature and fabric of it will begin to coalesce. With this ever-emerging clarity, we may well find ourselves increasingly paralyzed but subsequently awed by both the size and gravity of it. It's imperative that we understand that what we are seeking is decidedly bigger than the sum total of who we are. In fact, if we dare to explore it fully it will eventually tower over us, for anything less is less than a purpose. It's big because it's supposed to be. It's big because we were created big.

Therefore, the immensity of a purpose too often dictates the intensity with which we are prone to flee it. Yet, if we understand that we are explicitly built to perfectly mesh with this gloriously enormous thing that we call 'purpose', we begin to understand that we are finally at home in way we've never been at home before. We sit with something huge because we are created by a God who is huger still. Therefore, to be paralyzed by the size is to miss the fact that a purpose is not to be managed. It is to be done. It's not to be sized up. It's to be lived out. And once we're there, the size of our purpose becomes utterly exhilarating instead of profoundly intimidating.

To Not Seek Out Your Purpose is Only to Exist

Yet, many choose not to believe that they have a purpose, or they believe that they have one but don't bother themselves with finding it. There are those of us who succumb to a life of mindless tedium, or a pathetic routine where we senselessly march in lockstep with a world around us that's forsaken its purpose as well. There are those of us who readily embrace the pabulum of mediocrity which declares that things are about as good as they can get, so we'd better just settle for what we've got.

We surrender to a purposeless existence which is surrendering to death way ahead of death's actual arrival. And the sad story around all of this is that the majority of people will walk the journey of life down a road flat, never ascending, and rarely challenging. Many of us will know nothing other than a directionless cadence, having left the footprints of our lives meandering down a road that's meandering itself. Eventually the road will lead to wherever apathy and mediocrity pave it. And we can be certain that it will never lead to whatever our purpose was.

Your Purpose Awaits

You have a purpose. Despite your low estimation of yourself, you have a purpose. It stands eager and ready to be discovered. Purpose is never going to be so elusive that you can't find it simply because purpose is deeply desirous of being found, seized, unleashed and ultimately achieved. In doing so, you will change your life and the lives of those around you, because when you embrace your purpose nothing less than change can happen. If you don't seize your purpose, you will live out an anemic life and the world will be the poorer for it. Your existence will be of marginal effect, if any effect at all. And that reality is nothing short of tragic. It's time to ask one of the largest questions that you will ever ask yourself. And that question is, "What is my purpose?" The fact that you exist endows you with the right to ask that question. So, let's begin shaping and exploring that question.

The Hard Questions:

1. It's likely that you've thought about your purpose even though you may have written it off as impossible or the stuff of dreams. However, take a

minute and reclaim that for a moment.

2. Now that you have it, take a moment and define it more thoroughly. Identify it more specifically.

3. Now ask how this can be done...not how it can't. What steps could be taken, despite how small, that would move toward the fulfillment of this purpose?

Chapter Seven
Self-Esteem
The Five Big Lies

"Indeed, the very hairs of your head are all numbered. Don't be afraid; you are worth more than many sparrows."
-    Luke 12:7 (NIV)

"A man cannot be comfortable without his own approval."
-    Mark Twain

To get anywhere worth going we must navigate the barriers, for they will be there. Whether the challenge is large or small there will always be barriers. That is not a commentary on our worth or lack thereof. Rather, that is just a fact of life. Some of these barriers are small, seeming to demand little effort of us. Others are monstrous, leaving us paralyzed as we slowly back away from them in dismay and fear. Such is life and such is our response to them. If in fact there are no barriers, then the truth of the matter is that we are not going anywhere, for the barriers themselves evidence our momentum or lack thereof. Life is full of barriers, for without them life would be void of challenges and subsequently we would be void of growth.

Of all the manner of barriers, likely the single largest barrier to our ability to embrace great things is our own self-esteem. Such a barrier is formidable. The seemingly indiscriminate power of our self-image infiltrates every aspect of our psyche and every sphere of our lives. There is nowhere where it does not exist, and there is no instance where we are not touched by it. We are vigorously elevated by its power, or if turned against us we find ourselves in a blistering free-fall in the face of it. Anything that we attempt will be leveraged good or ill by the nature of our self-esteem.

The sad fact is that most times our self-esteem is damaged, egregiously wounded or crushed altogether. It walks with a limp, it instantly shies away from anything that would wound it any further and it spends most of its time withdrawing from everything instead of engaging anything. In whatever state our self-esteem happens to be in, more often than not it's something akin to this. And this is one of the greatest barriers of all.

Salvaging Our Low Self-Esteem by Blaming

Our reaction to a barrier such as this is to blame our failures on circumstances beyond our control or point out the unfairness of others or chalk it all up to the whimsy of fate. We point the finger at the fact that the timing was all wrong, the resources that should have been ours have been withheld from us, or we weren't meant for all of this in the first place. We proclaim luck gone sour, friends gone running and opportunity gone flat. Yet, looming behind the convincing facades and the well-crafted excuses that keep the facades erect there lies a weak and anemic self-esteem. It's not that 'others' kill us. It's that we kill ourselves.

What Is Self-Esteem?
Self-esteem is the accumulation of assorted beliefs that we have collected about ourselves. It's the messages of others crafted and shaped into hardened beliefs about who we are and who we are not. It's the collection of assorted perspectives that define what we see in the mirror at those times that we've been brave enough to look into it. In time, these become the immovable reality of our existence.

We arrange these many beliefs into some sort of piecemeal composite, much like a tile mosaic. Each piece is some shard lifted from some experience or encounter or event or circumstance or relationship that has come our way at some time in our lives. They are the product of painful family dynamics, soured social occurrences, relational upheavals, career disappointments, financial failures, and other things that package within themselves some distilled message about us. Some of these pieces are little more than miniscule fragments. Others are monstrous blocks. Rarely are any of them good.

A Deceived Self-Esteem

The key is that these many pieces are selected based on the belief that they are true about us, that whatever they represent about who we are is real and factual. We lend them an indisputable credibility when they are rarely credible. They become the fact of who we are that was drawn from the fiction projected on us by others, or the traits emblazoned on our character by the backlash of circumstance.

What we have yet to understand is that these pieces are more often a projection of the person or the situation that handed these pieces to us. They are what others found undesirable and wished to discard. So, rather than discard them, they made them about us. In a rather shrewd and somewhat ingenious manner, they were not ridding themselves of anything. Rather, they were just putting something where they felt it belonged. So, they made something belong to us that in fact belonged to them.

To make it stick, they diligently work to make us believe that these things belong to us. These people work to thoroughly convince us that they're not giving these issues to us nor are they passing them off on us. Rather, being led to believe that they were ours all along, we end up taking them from the others as if we're responsibly retrieving something that we lost along the way. An exchange of this manner creates a deceptively convincing shift, leading both parties to believe that the fault lies where in fact it does not. In essence, we're duped. We're fooled. We diligently collect these lies, tediously assemble them, and from them we build this rather convincing mosaic of who we are not.

In time, whether that be rapidly or somewhat slowly, we become completely convinced of each piece's authenticity. Despite innumerable circumstances that would pointedly and rather aggressively prompt us to do so, we are never even remotely moved to question its accuracy. It just becomes what over time it has just become. We rarely ask if this is who we are, for the question seems more a denial of who we are verses a genuine question of who we are.

Instead, we embrace this rankly naïve acceptance and therefore focus almost entirely on how to make the pieces work the best that we can. We live out 'what we are not' because we've lost 'who it is that we are.' We channel the messages until we live in a channel that we can't get out of. And we become so lost in this disjointed and dispirited mosaic that we no longer even realize that we are lost, which is just about as lost as anyone can ever hope to get.

Therefore, this mosaic, which is intended to be an accurate self-portrait of the person is nothing of the kind, although we are firmly convinced that it is so. Because it's often the projection of others or the labeling of circumstances, this mosaic tends to diminish us, often horribly and sometimes horrendously. It creates an ever-evolving picture that is more a mosaic of tarnished and discarded pieces rather than being a genuine reflection of who we truly are. And because we know no other course of action, we act out the mosaic in every dimension of life, allowing it to become a self-fulfilling and negatively reinforcing prophecy of everything that we are not.

Over time, I have discovered five lies that can wreck an individual's self-esteem and skew this mosaic. Five lies that hold a power to shape our lives to the destruction of our lives. These five lies impact our lives in profound ways and leave us impoverished in the living of our lives:

Lie#1 – Projection and Labeling As Facts

There are things that we don't like about ourselves. There are things about ourselves that frighten us to a point of incapacitating paralysis, that utterly crush fragile self-images, that descend upon us with inescapable pain, that wreck relationships and that leave us awash in a tidal pool of everything bad and nothing good. But when our attempts to deny their existence fails and the reach of these things are beyond the length of our stride, we seek relief by making these issues about someone else.

Therefore, we anxiously seek out someone who is relationally positioned to us in just such a manner that these issues could convincingly be seen as theirs. Or, we seek out someone quite distant from us whose behaviors, or lifestyle, or life circumstances are such that it would not be inconceivable that these issues could be theirs as well. Or we take editorial license and we craft some rather shrewd narrative that recasts someone in a manner that these issues seamless fit in their lives versus originating in ours. In whatever way we happen to do it we project our issues on someone else, thereby handily unburdening us of everything that haunts us.

Or, the reverse is true: as outlined previously, someone does this to us. When that happens, the issue is that we rather naïvely (and sometimes rather exuberantly) accept the behaviors, or the traits, or the qualities that are errantly attributed to us by others. We too often assume them to be ours and then we convince ourselves of them by living them out as if they were. Projection and labeling are not facts about who we are. They are not our story. They are the realities of another story made 'fiction' in our life so that the author can attempt to flee the 'facts' that they cannot flee.

We are not the landfill of frightened people nor are other people our landfill. We are not the whipping boy of all the people who are on the run from themselves and no one is that for us. We are not the story of someone else's failure and we can't pass our story along to someone else either. We are a unique and bold story written and being written on pages held by no one else except ourselves. We must respect that for ourselves as well as everyone around us.

Lie #2 - A Blatant Omission

Somehow, someway, for some inexplicable reason we bypass the good that we do. We assume the good to be the norm, the right thing to do, the thing for which no applause is warranted. It doesn't show up on our radar screens because it's not about some sort of extra or extended effort. It's not about the extra mile. It has nothing to do with the sacrifice or the cost incurred in sacrificing. It's just what we're all supposed to do. It's the norm. So why pay attention to what you're supposed to be doing in the first place?

Add to that the fact that good needs no further attention because good is good. What's there to work on? How do you build on good when it's already good? Focusing on the good sometimes seems a bit egocentric, so we pass it off in favor of everything that's not so good.

99

Therefore, we pay the good little to no attention; it just is. Consequently, any shard of good tends not to show up in the mosaic we are creating. In the end, this mosaic is often bereft of the very things that make us good, keep us good, and eventually make us great.

The priceless key is that the good that we do represents the good that we are. It's a manifestation of core traits that are marvelous and at times glorious. Our goodness is our greatness revealed. But we let our goodness fall to the bane of obscurity because the acts that were a manifestation of that priceless good are deemed as an irrelevant norm that holds nothing of value. And in such an errant action we forsake this magnificent good within us.

Lie #3 - We Rigorously Collect Flaws

Flaws become our focus. We literally fixate on them because they tell us that we are everything that they are, and that they are everything that we are. They lay a stern and often unchallenged claim to the whole of our identity, stating that there is nothing else beside them. Our flaws seem to seek a prominence in our lives, deceptively declaring that our identity is what we have to fix, not what we have to celebrate. As such, they scream for our attention and we give them plenty of it because in time we believe that there's no other part of ourselves to give attention to.

The presence of our flaws assumes the absence of anything good, or at least the absence of anything sufficiently good. Over time, our flaws lead us to embrace the belief that anything good within us is itself a flaw in our thinking. Anything good was an accident not likely to happen again, a misstep that we can't take credit for because there was nothing intentional in the action, or the success of another that we indirectly took as our own. We can't be trusted to understand anything about ourselves because any such thinking is likely to be flawed as well. And in the end, the only thought that we have any confidence in is that we're flawed.

Obviously, we want to fix these flaws but we often feel that we can't because we're flawed. We feel too flawed to fix our flaws. We're then trapped and stymied, caught dead-center in the very thing we feel we can't solve. With the good in us largely unrecognized and being held captive to everything we abhor about us, our flaws are free to roam throughout every corner of our lives. And in the relentless roaming, they completely define us. As much as we hate it, they end up dominating our mosaic, painting these pictures in pasty grays and washes of jet black.

Lie #4 - Flaws Reinforced

If that's not bad enough, we hear about our flaws

from others, whether it's from a parent or a spouse or a sibling or a boss or a teacher or some stranger. Our ethnicity is attacked. Our occupation is degraded. Our successes are drawn through the rank mud of criticism. We become the stereotype of the issues projected upon us. We become the narrative of those running from themselves. We become the poster child of their fears as they've been dumped on us. Within whatever circles they travel and in whatever frightened hovels they live, the stories of us are passed on as a means of convincing others that the fiction about us is the fact that defines us. In creating these 'alliances of lies' where others sit and nod in ignorant agreement, these stories are accepted as our story.

And whether it be in close proximity or at some distance, it is likely that as some point and in some place we will intersect one or more of these unfortunate and rather gullible people. And like some airborne virus, they will carry this fictional story to us. And when they do, they will deliver it through the rendition born of their lenses and groomed by their ignorance, leaving it sufficiently intact but adding enough dynamics to lend it an even greater edge.

Who it comes from matters some, but not much. The fact is that our flaws are reinforced by others who are likely running from their own flaws. The story is told, retold and recast in the telling. It is reinforced and finds a false legitimacy. And after we are sufficiently pummeled by these encounters we find ourselves increasingly unsettled, leaving room for doubt to seep into the crevices of our insecurities. In its devious and stealthy way, a lie reinforced can begin to look like a truth told. And when they are told, we desperately hope that they aren't true. However, we must always remember that no amount of reinforcement will ever make a lie the truth. Ever.

Lie #5 – I Was Born Flawed

Really? The ultimate surrender is in believing that we were born flawed. Somehow our nature is assumed to be inherited much like our hair color or shoe size. It just is. Genetics got us. We just happened to be at the shallow end of the gene pool when things were being handed out. We ended up in 'that' kind of family. Whatever the behaviors are that resulted in 'that' kind of family, every single one of those unsavory traits runs dead-center through every generation right down to us and we have no place to hide. We're stuck with whatever we perceive our inherent flaws to be whether inherited or adopted. The only option that we have is to manage our flaws as best we can, hoping against hope that we can at least do something marginally good with our lives.

Fate has laid these things upon us, or so we think. Sometimes we view our presumed flaws as a dreaded reality that we cannot escape, the result of a litany of happenstance events that preceded our existence and will be carried out throughout the entirety of our existence right through the end. We see ourselves as the product of fate, chance, circumstance, providence or whatever other rather ethereal thing we've come to call it.

All of this grants us permission to not try so that, should we fail in the trying, we won't reinforce the failures we believed ourselves to be. We don't want to give it a shot because we don't want to be left looking in some lonely mirror telling ourselves "I told you so." With our self-esteem as low as it is, we've already spent plenty of time doing that. At other times we're just plain apathetic because we haven't found any other viable alternative.

Regardless, we are not born failures. We become them. And when we become failures, we are failures in our heads and not in our make-up. Failure is not who we are. It's what we do. Failure is the fiction that will never be anything other than fiction. We're human of course, we will make mistakes. Lots of mistakes. However, most of these flaws were not originally part of the mosaic. We put them in, or we gave other's permission to insert them. But born this way you were not.

Think About It

You are what you choose to be. Life is not a dictated script. It's far from being something to which you have to surrender. Yes, there are things that we did not ask for that we have to deal with. Regardless, whatever our flaws there is always room to do something about them. Always. Some option always exists. There are always possibilities. Life affords us choices and chances. The human spirit is tenacious, powerful and wonderfully creative. Don't underestimate your capabilities and your resources. Realize that the resources that you possess outclass and outweigh any flaw, whether perceived or real. You can wound magnificence, but magnificence only becomes more magnificent in the wounding. Choose to view yourself in a new way, differently and more accurately. Choose to choose you, for despite your low self-esteem, you won't be disappointed.

The Hard Questions:
1. Pick your largest flaw and ask what you want to do about it.
2. Whatever it is that you want to do about it, pick one positive attribute that you have that will help in that task.
3. Once you've determined a positive attribute, apply it to your flaw every day.

Chapter Eight
I Am Only One
Understanding Our Impact

"I looked for someone among them who would build up the wall and stand before me in the gap on behalf of the land so I would not have to destroy it, but I found no one."
- Ezekiel 22:30 (NIV)

"I am only one but still I am one. I cannot do everything, but still I can do something."
- Edward Everett

I am only one. That's all I am. I am only one and I will always be only one. I was born as one, I will live as one, and on the day of my death I will die as one. In this journey that we all call life, I am and will always be completely restricted and wholly limited to being one and only one. I can stand shoulder-to-shoulder with a thousand people, but I am still only one among a thousand. And all of those daunting realities strike me as miserably pathetic and colossally discouraging. Sadly, I am only one.

I am only one in a mammoth sea of surging and foaming humanity within which my main and often single goal is simply to survive. The winds will blow and the tides will roll in whatever way they spuriously and often callously choose to blow and roll. The challenges will rise and the darkness will fall. Enemies will advance against me and mountains will rise in front of me. People will embrace me out of a love potent beyond words, and at other times they will backstab me out of an evil dark beyond comprehension. And whatever choices life (in all its assorted forms) will make will dictate the ways that I will go because I'm far too small to swim against them, and far too weak to even dare chart a different course from theirs. I am only one and being one doesn't appear to be enough.

I am only one, and because I am, even the reality of my existence is of little note. In the span of this minute, or this hour, or this day, or in the span of history itself my existence will not only be largely disregarded, it won't even register enough to acknowledge that I was here in the first place. Even the briefest notation that I have made or will make on the pages of history will be entirely lost in the seemingly infinite volumes of tightly written copy that stretch from mankind's earliest moments to his eventual demise because I am only one.

Eventually my life will be relegated to the stuff of memory held in photos, kept in yellowed letters, resurrected in fuzzy recollections and spoken of when the ever-decreasing opportunities present themselves to do so. The one that I am will soon cease to be except for the occasional memory that somehow randomly surfaced. Being only one seems entirely insufficient in and of itself. But worse yet, it will someday soon cease to be even that. And so, I am only one who is doomed to soon be even less than that.

Living as Being Only One
And so, because I am only one, I relegate myself to being only one. I surrender to this weak singularity. I am obscure, so much so that I can hardly define myself or my purpose as held against the billions of others within which my existence becomes swallowed up and lost. I am an unrecognizable anomaly in the forever thread of history. The accumulation of eons of time leaves me awash in an existence so vast that my presence or absence within it makes no difference. As held against history, time and creation, I will enter with barely a sound and I will exit in the same manner. And so, I hope to experience a bit of joy, touch a few other lives whose lives will likewise fall to the peril of being only one, laugh a little here and there and then be gone. For it seems that is the best that I can hope to hope for.

The Potential of Being One
And in relegating myself to being one and only one, I unwittingly embrace the limitations that I perceive as being part and parcel of being one and only one. I become staunchly convinced of what I think being one means and subsequently what it does not mean. I suit-up in the pathetic apparel of powerlessness, I chart a path of capitulation that's dictated by the insensitive winds and tides of life and I bow to the

lamentable goal of surrender because I figure that that's about as good as it gets.

But this whole thing of being only one is appreciably compounded by the fact that I don't believe in this one that I am. It's limiting enough just being one in this assorted mass of moving humanity. But when the one that I am doesn't appear to meet even the most minimal threshold of whatever being one should be, I feel a whole lot more like nothing.

Recognizing the fact that I'm one but feeling like I'm nothing discounts the one that I am, as small as that one might be. Therefore, it would have been far, far better being nothing to begin with as I can't be anything less than that. Being nothing gives me a legitimate reason to feel like I'm nothing because that's what I am, when being at least one would suggest that I'm something. And then I trail off on this destructive thought that it would have been better had I not existed at all for that would dispense with any tangled debate regarding the illegitimacy of my existence.

One Plus...

I staunchly hold to the 'gospel of one' within which I believe that my oneness is lived out in oneness. Through this isolation of self as being only unto self and nothing else, I have bound myself with the limitations of myself. I have played out the dismal scenarios in the confines of this singular rubric that define who I am. I assume that the equation of this one that I am is an equation that has no external factors against which it can multiplied. One times one is one. Always and forever.

Therefore, any evaluation of who I am is held to the sparseness of who I am, without understanding that who I am in union with Who God is renders me capable of being everything that I am not. I have yet to understand that my oneness is never held solely to itself. Life is a corporate deal, whether you believe in God or not. That corporate quality is reflected in nature's dependence upon everything else in nature as one mammoth interactive ecosystem that constantly builds all the parts of itself as it builds the whole of itself. That ecosystem is the manifestation of a God's character. That's the beauty of a God Who recognized that the experience of anything living in isolation would be limited to that to which it is isolated. Life is too rich to miss the majority of it by having lived in some small sliver of it. One times an infinite God is infinity. Always and forever.

The Seeds in My Oneness
Therefore my oneness is the seed of a greater greatness. That when my oneness is joined with God, with those others He brings alongside me, with the dreams He has implanted within me, within the purpose He has destined me for, this one will remain one but it will be a one that has moved leagues

beyond its own oneness. I am one, but I am not one in isolation. Rather, I am one that when brought together with other ones and empowered by the Great One will experience a manifestation far beyond this one that I am. In essence, my one remains one but becomes far more than one.

The Fear of Understanding

But I don't understand any of that. Or worse yet, I don't believe it. Or worse beyond that, I don't want to understand it for fear that I might believe it. My oneness is utterly convinced of its oneness and it lives in a panicked fear that attempting to be anything other than one is to have that one crushed in a disappointment so deep that it will never recover. The conviction of the belief that I am only one has firmly established itself as my immovable reality. As such, I have settled into this belief and shaped every element of my life around it. And I live out my days and sort out my life in this suffocating oneness because it has become the definition of who I am and what life is.

And then in some sort of tense angst, I hunker down and wait for whatever's going to happen to me, letting my mind spin in wild gyrations as I frantically attempt to figure out how I'm going to deal with whatever's going to happen when it eventually happens. Being only one means that the odds will always be against me. I will always stand in an inferior position. I will live forever in the throes of fight-versus-flight because I am not enough to do otherwise. I will never possess the power to survive or thwart the forces that come against me as they will always be greater than me. In a larger sense, we are all one and therefore we are all subject to and helpless before whatever might befall us. And this becomes the story that I believe and the story that I live. And in this kind of story, my self-esteem simply doesn't have a chance.

What Does Being One Really Mean?

What will I do with the fact that I am only one? I am only one in a world that's spiraling. I am only one in a world that's rapidly recreating itself in garments that are far from the ethics, morals and values within which it was clothed at birth. I am only one in a culture that's lost its moorings and is finding itself on a dangerously churning sea that the culture has cleverly labeled "progressive" or "cutting-edge" or "liberal thinking" in order to avoid the implications of living on such perilous seas. I am only one in a world driven by the insatiable gluttony of selfishness rather than the spirited nourishment that comes from selfless living and self-effacing choices. I am only one in all of that.

I stand as only one in the face of forces that only seem to gain momentum as they gorge themselves on our world. I can turn in every direction and find injustice, prejudice, hatred, greed, and power-mongering. I can watch lives being swallowed up in the gore of their own decisions or destroyed by the thoughtless decisions of others. Divorce proliferates. Betrayal runs rampant. Disease moves about unchecked. Addictions steal jobs, press relationships to ruin, unleash confusion and kill. Godless agendas promise everything and deliver everything except everything. And in the toxic swill of all of this, I am only one. Just one. And how is that single singularity supposed to be able to do anything?

But I Am One

But I am one, and that is infinitely better than being "none." I am one, which puts me on equal footing with everyone else. Every single person in human history who impacted history in ways either large or small faced the same exact dilemma that I am faced with: they were one and no more than one. I am only one, but I do not stand as empty or hollow or void. Quite the opposite. This one that I am comes tightly packaged with innumerable gifts, talents and abilities that stand at the ready. I am only one, but that one that I am is entirely and irrevocably different from any other "one" that has ever lived in the entire expanse of human history. I am only one, but I have inspiring dreams and vitally rich visions for life that are unlike those held by anyone else. I am only one, but I have unbridled access to everyone other 'one' around me. I am only one, but I live with a God Who is the infinite One. Oh yes, I am only one, but I am 'one.'

The Opportunity in Being "One"

I am unbelievably privileged to be one, particularly the one that I am. I don't think I'd really want it any other way. But I only get one shot at being one. I get this single, sole opportunity to take this one that I am and use it to make a difference in all the other 'ones' around me. I have the privilege of impacting the ones around me, who will in turn impact other ones, who will in turn impact yet other ones . . . and on it goes. I can be one person who impacts the world 'one' person at a time, and in doing so I can potentially impact all of the other ones in all of the world. That's not a bad deal. So, I'd be wise to take advantage of this one and only one shot I get at being this 'one' that I am.

It might be wise to consider that I am only one, yet I live in a world of ones. That means that I am uniquely suited to impact other ones like me. I am what they are. They are what I am. We are all the same. And because that's the case, I have the unique advantage of speaking into their lives because I'm living out their lives, and they're living out mine. Our existence is shared, our experiences are similar, our joys are pretty much the same and our pain is familiar to all of us. We walk through the same life, with the same experiences and the same challenges as this one and only one person that we all are. And being one like everybody else, I am perfectly suited to speak directly into the lives of all the other ones around me. So, why don't I?

The Fears of Being "One"

The Fear of Not Being Enough
I think that we fear that being one is not enough. Being one is too often seen as being inadequate. The world out there is not some massive mass of people. It is a collection of individuals. It's a bunch of 'ones.' By and large, those individuals experience life pretty much the same way that we do. It's all just a collection of 'ones.' It's a collection of people that are each one individual just like we are one person. While being one makes us perfectly suited to impact all the other ones around us, we still fear that being one is not enough.

The Fear that We Can't be Loud Enough
I also think that we fear that our single voice is not loud enough. We don't have the volume to be heard over the raucous roar and interminable noise in our world. We can't possibly scream loud enough or long enough to be heard in the ruckus and racket that defines the world around us. So our voices are drowned out. Yet, we need to remember that we're not speaking to the world around us. We're speaking to the ones around us. And because that's the case, there's plenty of them and we're plenty loud enough.

The Fear of Being Rejected
I think that maybe our greatest fear is that we will be heard, and that in being heard we'll be rejected or

discounted or blown off. It seems that our single biggest fear is rejection. What if we're heard and in the hearing we're labeled as stupid, naïve or ignorant? What if we're heard and then we're slapped with accusations of being politically incorrect, culturally ill-informed, biased, mistaken at some fundamental level or something of a faith-based moron? What if we take a stand? What if we refuse to compromise? What if we speak against the toxicity that's seeping into the lives around us? What if what we're saying isn't popular or trendy or it's absent in the talking points of a screaming media? What if? I think that we need to understand that there are 'ones' out there who share our convictions and who understand the oppressive burdens that birthed those convictions. Indeed, we are 'one' but we are not alone in being 'one.'

The Fear of Failure
What if I step out as one in the midst of the chaos and the darkness and the malaise, and what if I fail? What if nothing is different? What if I am shamed into submission as my failures bring me face-to-face with the limitations of being only 'one' that I hoped were not true? What if I try and nothing changes? What if I step up and get knocked down? Then through some misplaced hope and fanciful zeal I have done nothing other than convince myself that being only 'one' is truly limited to being only 'one.' That my life will expend itself in the expending of itself with nothing to show for it. And I hardly think

that I could live with that.

The Fear of Responsibility

But what if this one that I am is not a one in isolation? What if I can change things? What if I can impact the world? What if? Maybe we don't want to be responsible for that much power. Maybe we don't want to shoulder some sort of bold mantle, draw our resources around us and press out against so much of what is destroying so many. Maybe under the right circumstances we'd be willing to following someone who would do that, but we don't want to be the one doing that. We prefer to leave such exploits to others and follow them at a comfortable distance or track them from afar. But, what if we actually pull it off and are left with the responsibility of having done that? The responsibility might be a bit too much for us.

The Opportunity of Being "One"

I am only one in a mammoth sea of surging and foaming humanity within which my main and often single goal is simply to survive. But I am one, and my oneness is sufficient to forgo surviving and embrace living. The winds will blow and the tides will roll in whatever way they spuriously and often callously choose to blow and roll. And whatever choice they make does not have to dictate the ways that I will go because I am one, and because I am I can swim against them and dare to chart a different course from theirs. I am only one and despite the rather lackluster view of myself, being one is enough.

I am only one, and because I am, the reality of my existence can change the reality of everyone around me. In the span of this minute, or this hour, or this day, or in the span of history itself my existence can be noted, and because I am one it can register enough to acknowledge that I was here. The briefest notations that I have made or will make on the pages of history will add moving lines of inspiration in the seemingly infinite volumes of tightly written copy that stretch from mankind's earliest moments to his eventual demise because I am one.

I am in union with the Infinite 'One' Who renders me capable of being everything that I am not. I have yet to understand that my oneness is never held solely to itself. That my oneness is the seed of a greater greatness that when joined with God, with those others He brings alongside me, with the dreams He has implanted within me, with the purpose He has bestowed upon me will remain one, but it will be a one that has moved leagues beyond its own oneness. Yes, I am only one, but I am one in league with a God Who makes my oneness infinite. I am only one but being only one is more than enough.

You have one chance at being 'one.' You have been granted one life to touch the other 'ones' around you. Being one is being enough. Life's about being intentional about being the best 'one' that you can be, and intentionally touching all the other ones around you in a manner that transforms them 'one' at a time. In transforming the ones in our world we will eventually transform our world. So, go be the one that you are. Step up in a world that's spiraling, confront a culture that has remodeled itself, and seize the tattered lines of a nation that has lost its moorings. Be the one that you were designed to be and change the world by being that one, for despite your poor assessment of yourself you will always remain this beautiful one.

The Hard Questions:

1. As being only one, how would describe that 'one' person that you are?

2. As you think about being that one person, what parts of that person are capable of having an impact outside of that person?

3. What parts of that person when put into the hands of God have the potential of transforming people for eternity?

Chapter Nine
Cultivating the Good
The Great Stories Within Us

"Very truly I tell you, whoever believes in me will do the works I have been doing, and they will do even greater things than these, because I am going to the Father."
-    John 14:12 (NIV)

"One's only rival is one's own potentialities. One's only failure is failing to live up to one's own possibilities. In this sense, every man can be a king, and must therefore be treated like a king."
-    Abraham Maslow

Mankind's history is strewn with sordid stories of horrific evil. The yellowed pages of history as well as the fresh pages of the daily paper are littered thick and scattered knee deep with accounts of ruthless destruction, mindless devastation, heartless obliteration and acts so viciously awful that they are at times entirely incomprehensible. We witness the mindless actions of hearts gone rogue where families are destroyed or communities are left roiling in smoke and ash. We can cull through the endless annals of history and find them brimming with evil acts both large and small. At the end of any day we can pull up the news of the past twenty-four hours and find them saturated with the very same evil often carried out in the very same way. Evil

120

abounds.

Human beings are completely capable of envisioning a sordid array of horrendous acts and then constructing inherently devious ways to execute them with cold, calculated impunity. It seems that the ability of mankind to creatively and effectively devise ways to maim, kill and torrentially rain all kinds of destruction on others is nothing short of boundless. Destruction is genius misdirected or insanity let loose. That edge where morality gives way to immorality teases many to skirt its treacherous escarpment, with most never coming back from the fall.

But when there is a premeditated intentionality to such actions, and when the targeting is purposeful and calculated, such behaviors terrorize our sense of self and victimize our sense of worth. It's people armed with dark intent and we're in the crosshairs. It's those who plot great evil in the deep recesses of minds gone dark, refining their plans to maximize the blow that they are about to inflict upon us. There's some sense that the destruction of others enhances the pleasure of the one doing the destroying. Therefore, they're always planning more. That kind of intentional evil seems violently elevated with no peak in the elevation. Aimed at us, it destroys our sense of self, leaving us wandering the bleeding barrens of self-hatred.

Evil in Our Faces
The ability to coldly and effectively destroy others, as well as the many devious and varied ways that destruction of that kind is carried out, is liberally splashed across the screens and scrolling pages of much of the media, gorging us on a daily diet of this most dark side of mankind. These acts are often spun in captivating images and gripping language that sometimes seems more designed to generate a viewership rather than objectively and reverently communicate a tragedy. These situations are often dissected, parsed, analyzed and scrutinized to death out of a misguided commitment to thorough journalism that is too often propelled by the need to compete with all the other branches of the media that are all following the same story. Evil can author a compelling script that's offered the platform of high definition, high speed internet, iPads and surround sound.

Regardless, in light of a tragedy the inherent focus becomes the act of evil. Indeed, evil is captivating. It dares us to touch the forbidden and tentatively come out and play with the darker side of ourselves. Evil tickles our curiosity and bids us to take a slight step closer. It teases us with the idea that we can touch it yet not become engulfed in it.

Evil tells us that we're better than all the others who brushed up against it and were

122

swallowed up by it. It wants us to believe that we can view it up close, run a slight bit of it through our fingers, catch a faint aroma of its scent and look it in the eye, all as some sort of entertaining amusement from which we walk away unscathed. Evil presents itself as harmless and as something on innocent display, not as something that seeks to put us on display by locking us in a cage of its own making. All of this makes it intriguing, tantalizing and enticing. Therefore, despite our frequent aversion to it, we become captivated by it.

Evil in Our Faces Leaves the Good Missed
In the expanding and sometimes engulfing focus on evil, we miss the good as any good is relentlessly marginalized and ignorantly shoved off into lonely corners. The greatest evil of all is that which has convinced us that evil is the sum total of our existence. That good is a myth of static idealists, or it's too weak to do anything other than die the instant that it's born, or it's yet another ruse of evil itself playing with gullible minds. For those of us with low self-esteem, we don't see any good within ourselves anyway, so this kind of evil only serves to confirm what we believe to be true about ourselves.

The Characteristics of Good as Held Against Evil
Evil is completely brazen. Good is quietly subtle. Evil is tantalizing. Good is emboldening. Evil is something that calls us to deceptive play. Good calls

us to hard and sweaty sacrifice. Evil makes no demands that we step up. Good is all about stepping up...over and over. Evil tells us that our agenda rules and that we have unrestrained permission to gorge ourselves sick on whatever that agenda desires. Good tells us that our agenda is the agenda of the person next to us. Evil dares us to dance on the fine line of right and wrong, seeing how good we are at playing both sides of that line. Good demands that we relentlessly hold the line.

Evil soothes our pricked and irritated consciences by ceaselessly handing out an endless array of justifications and rationalizations that effectively neutralize anything that might be unethical about those actions. Good relentlessly calls us to accountability, abjectly refusing to hand us free passes for poor choices and unethical decisions. Evil markets itself as easy, unobtrusive and permissive. Good refuses compromise, it makes no bones about what it demands and it will not bend to the spin of marketing.

Evil will lead us to believe that it's not evil at all, but rather it's simply an emancipating expression of our inherent liberties. It tells us that evil unrestrained is really just our inner selves finally finding some breathing room. It leads us to believe that it's only evil because some self-proclaimed righteous individual labeled it as such and unfortunately, the label stuck. Evil will whisper in our ears that thinking about whether we matter doesn't matter because nothing does. Therefore, to be free is to accept that reality and walk in the liberty of it. And despite all of the subtly twisted messages, good simply stands as good. Clearly however, evil has quite a degree of appeal. So, it gets plenty of attention.

What We're Capable Of

Because evil has a captivating appeal, it too often has the focus as well. Because it does, we miss the ability of mankind to perform incredible acts of valor and monumental actions of unimaginable sacrifice. We forget the inherent good within us that causes us to step up at tremendous risk to ourselves in order to eliminate the risk faced by another. There is within us a curiously intrinsic instinct to ensure the good of others that supersedes our own safety. There's something tightly woven throughout the fabric of our humanity that runs entirely opposite to the baser instinct of looking out for our own good. We have within us the ability to put ourselves directly in harm's way in order to rescue others. There is something within us that rises far above our own sense of self and calls us to throw self-preservation to the wind and subsequently do things we could not have imagined that we were capable of doing.

When called up either intentionally or by circumstance, the good within us can handily overcome the evil within us and around us.

Therefore, the far, far greater part of our humanity is good regardless of the immensity of any tragedy. The problem seems to be that the good is too often submerged by inattention and subverted by lies. In a culture that tends to focus on the evil within it, the good is not sufficiently cultivated because it's sufficiently hidden and ignorantly ignored. We seem to have forsaken something wildly deep, incredibly strong and relentlessly relentless. We have opted to toy with evil as some entrancing thing and to be entertained by its endless exploits. In doing that, we've turned our attention away from the greater good that is a far greater part of our humanity.

The Great Stories of Great Good

In any tragedy there are endless stories of those who stood in the face of great danger on behalf of someone else. There are those who instantaneously risked their lives for total strangers without taking the time to question what they were doing. There are those who out of a natural response of great good rushed to scenes of catastrophe and carnage in order to lend a hand, shield a body, bind a wound and share a heart. There are those forgotten and often invisible people who bolted out of the comfort and safety of their own lives to run directly into the smoke, ashes and flaming structures of the lives of others.

There are those who intentionally stepped in harm's way without so much as a thought, who slogged through the blood of others whether that blood ran from wounded bodies or was more the stuff of emotional blood that runs just as red and just as deep. There are people who acted out of a far greater instinct that called them to do something far greater than any evil could possibly hope to match. There are people who manifested good as part of the fullest manifestation of our corporate humanity.

Responding to the 'great good' within us causes us to be 'great people' because that 'great person' lays within us. We might not see it. Our battered self-esteem may no longer sense any hint of it. The pages of a tarnished history may evidence the absence of it. Regardless of how convincing, none of these invalidates the existence of a 'great good' within us.

Responding to the great good within us thrusts us up to who and what we were originally designed by God to be. By choice, we live terribly small lives that are constricted by fear and wrenched cold by our low self-esteem. Yet, tragedy beckons us to step up, leap out of those constraints and vault into our own fullness. It causes us to smash our pre-imposed boundaries and surge across our own superficial limits in the pursuit of our true design. Tragedy triggers the great good within us and unleashes it in ways that are so stunning that we run into the face of danger because inherently we know that it's the right thing to do. That reality of our 'great good' should be our focus.

At times of great tragedy, the ability to exhibit great good will always offset great evil despite how great that evil might be. That truth needs to be our focus in times of tragedy. That reality needs to be our belief in ourselves because in believing that we are acting on fact, not on a fit of desperate fantasy. Evil cannot be the focus. Rather, the focus must be the great good that always offsets it. That is not to say that we ignore evil or downplay it. Neither should we believe that we can neatly overcome it with some wave of our proverbial hand or wash it from our minds with a fresh set of constructive thoughts. Such beliefs would be naïve, foolish and dangerous.

Rather, it is to say that in the light of any tragedy large or small we need to be reminded yet again of the magnificently great good that unapologetically underlies each and every life and that staunchly undergirds every heart. We must understand that when cultivated and exercised, this good that God has placed within us can overcome the bad the world has sown around us. We cannot be dismayed and diminished in light of evil. Instead, we must be encouraged and emboldened by the good within each and every one of us that can offset every tragedy.

The Great Stories Within You

The 'great stories' are often attributed to other people living lives at some immense distance from ours. We see them as existing at other times or in other places that are just as distant. These stories and the people who live them out are removed from us at a distance so utterly vast that their dramas play themselves out in another reality that never intersects ours. We come to believe that our role is to be awed by their exploits and entertained in and by the telling of them because we are far too small for such stories. But as we discussed in the previous chapter, we might only be one. However, the people of the great stories were only one as well.

While we acknowledge that they are phenomenal stories, we become convinced that they are not our stories. We become entirely enraptured by them. We gladly acquiesce to their grandeur. We surrender our imagination to the acts of heroism and sacrifice. We are inspired in both the telling and the hearing of such tales. At times we insert ourselves into the story to bring some measure of relief to our boredom and grant ourselves a momentary reprieve from our own repetitive mediocrity. We participate as listeners only, being on the receiving end of the exploits of brave people living out the lives that we'd love to live out.

Yet, we haven't even stopped to consider the possibility that there are great stories within us. We don't consider the fact that the humanity that we carry within us holds the same God-given essence and character held by those who lived out these tales. We have yet to understand that the only difference between us and these people is that these people believed (or dared to believe) in that essence and that character enough to unleash it. They were 'us' cut loose. We don't understand that it's not that we lack anything, for we are as equipped and as fully sufficient for our calling as anyone else is for theirs. Rather, it's that we don't unleash it.

And so, we find it entirely implausible to believe that these stories are as much ours as anyone else's. We don't realize that we can live out the events that become the stories told by others. Our damaged self-esteem convinces us that we will always sit in the distant audience as passive listeners, forever envious of the tales spun by others. We believe that we will be active participants only in the sense that we can vicariously join through the hearing of the stories and the distant celebration of their glories. We can partner in the appreciation and applause of victories won, but we feel that we ourselves will never win them.

Celebrating Our Great Stories
But did God design any of us to be listeners only? Were we created to stand at some irreconcilable distance and do little more than applaud the stories of others, wipe a tear from eyes moved with emotion and leave to live out our lives wishing that we were

the stories? Is that the sum total of our existence? Is this our sorry lot in life? Is that the best that God can come up with for us?

Our low self-esteem tells us that we were made for the little stories that are in fact no story at all. The stuff that no one sees. The scripts that leave our hearts vanquished, the world unmoved and our legacy not worth the ink or the paper to write it out on. We don't have a story. Not a real one anyway. Those are for someone else. Those are for the capable people. The grand people. The beautiful people. The gifted people. The people called out and called up from the doldrums of plodding humanity.

But God wants us to know that with Him, we are capable. With Him we are grand. With Him we are beautiful. With Him we are gifted. With Him we are called out and called up not because humanity might be filled with plodding masses, but because God finds immeasurable pleasure in doing the impossible in the plodding masses through the frailty of our own humanity. And it is not about what we bring to all of us. It is about what God brings to all of 'us.' It's about the great good inherent within us that is begging to be unleashed outside of us.

Evil abounds. But you have a story greater than all the evil that will ever surround you. You have a story of victory. Of power. Of celebration. Of great joy and immeasurable wonder. At times it will be a story of great pain, unrelenting betrayal and mounting disappointment. But that's what the great good within us is designed to overcome. You have a great story because you have a great God Who is waiting for you to tell a story so great that you will become enraptured in the telling of it. This is your privilege. This is your right. This is your opportunity. This is your promise. This is you and it's for you.

Let's not let evil take center stage in our lives or in the world. May the great goodness of our great God as intricately woven into the very fabric of our souls be preeminent on the stage of any tragedy. May we begin to see our great goodness in the place where all we saw was our great nothingness. And may that great goodness be cultivated throughout our days whether those days are marked by tragedy or lived out in joy and bliss. Thank God for a great good that will never be beaten by any tragedy regardless of how great it might be.

The Hard Questions:
1. Identify the good within you. Once you do, consider the possibility that the good within you might be greater than you understand.
2. Begin to focus on the great good within you as you look at the great evil around you. Consider how that great good might overcome that evil if you unleash it.
3. Finally, are you willing to ask God for a great story

to live out? Not a mediocre story or one of your own composition, but a great story authored by God and fueled by the great good within you?

Chapter 10
We Are Better Than This
Missing the Essence of Us

"I praise you because I am fearfully and wonderfully made; your works are wonderful, I know that full well."
-    Psalm 139:14 (NIV)

"We are all strangers to our hidden potential until we confront problems that reveal our capabilities."
-    Apoorve Dubey

Rarely do we rise to the pinnacle of our capabilities. Most of those that we pass everyday will live out the entirety of their lives falling achingly short of what they could have been. There's little vision to see what they are, when there's plenty of vision to see what they're not. Sadly, there are far more assumptions regarding the existence of deficits than the belief in the presence of strengths. Too often we have come believe that our weaknesses are the essence of our character instead of the focus of our attention. People exist in the doldrums of passivity because there's no inherent belief that theirs is a life made for more. Lives are wasted with seeming impunity.

I can imagine few things as horrific as a life having played out the length of its years having fallen achingly short of the potential of its abilities. How

134

sad that the inherent qualities that jostle for release within us are not set free to create the person who was never meant to be anything other than free. And these sorts of tragedies are only exponentially compounded by the fact that there exists a myriad array of people whose lives could have been profoundly (and even radically) touched by this single life that chose not to live its life. Things such as this are inexcusable, but they are happening all of the time. And our task is to make certain that they are not happening to us.

Why We Fall Short
We may fall short of our abilities because we don't wish to expend the energy to do something so bold and flagrantly daring as to rise to the best of ourselves. Maybe we assume that an effort of that magnitude takes too much work, or the extent of the sacrifice is somehow inconvenient or uncomfortable or possibly excessive. Maybe comfort is our goal or ease in living is our cherished destination, therefore we are dead set on not disturbing any of that. Or maybe we don't believe that any such abilities exist within us and therefore a search for them is something akin to a search for some mythical creature of lore and legend. However, we are better than this.

As we noted, we may not believe that we possess any potential to rise to, therefore such an endeavor is futility at its finest. Maybe we've decided that the issue of settling is really more a matter of accepting who we are, but more importantly, who we're not (which becomes the definition of ourselves for ourselves). Maybe we find comfort in believing that there are those gifted others who will carry the load because they have been granted the ability to do so, thereby freeing us of something we can't do because we don't possess their abilities. Maybe we feel that asking the question regarding our capabilities is beyond our capabilities, so we don't ask the question and therefore we begin to die for lack of asking. However, we are better than this.

Or, in the larger scope of things we may view ourselves as so terribly irrelevant that it simply doesn't matter what we do or don't do. We are one of billions anyway. In the span of history we are a blip. An anomaly. A footnote that won't be noted. We are something of a nearly invisible irregularity that will pass without a nod or any sort of recognition whatsoever. Who we are is who we will not be because we will not be. The photos will be lost. The stories will fade. Recollections of a life lived will become the recollections of someone that no one can recall. And therefore we live out this life of silent desperation and no accord. Despite the exact nature of our particular orientation or the bruised condition of our self-esteem, the fact of the matter is that we are better than this.

Descending to Our Inabilities

Sadly, all too often we readily descend to the dismal pit of our inabilities. Descending to that pit is both easier to do and easier to believe in. It's what people have said that we are and where we belong, so it's simply a fulfillment of our sordid destiny. It demands little of us other than the wholesale abandonment of our abilities and subsequently the betrayal of our calling. It's the place from which failure is not possible because we believe that we have already failed to the fullest extent possible. Therefore, in some sad and pathetic sense it's safe. So, because the pit is easier on too many fronts, we find ourselves spending a lot of time in it to the point that we never leave it. However, we are better than this.

The Two Sides of Us
We're remarkably and gloriously human with all of the magnificent traits God has generously and ingeniously birthed into us. However, we're terribly primal at the same time. We can fall to our baser selves with relative ease, while rising to our greatest selves takes commitment, fortitude and energy. We can press up into something phenomenal, but we can spiral down into something putrid. We can be the hero or the hellraiser. The life-lifter or the life-leveler. Oddly enough, there exist within us these two entirely opposite, but strangely cooperative elements.

It is the worst of ourselves that calls out the

best of ourselves. It is the worst of ourselves that evidences the best of ourselves by setting itself up as opposite to that part of us. The worst of ourselves is the thing that incites the best of ourselves because somewhere we know that we are better than this. The worst of ourselves challenges the best of ourselves, incessantly shouting that the best of ourselves is a fantasy born of the need to believe that we're better than this. The worst of ourselves says that anything 'good' is a desperate narrative that we've crafted in order to believe that something within us somewhere has some shred of decency to it.

Think about it. We possess the ability to access an intellect that outside of God has no equal in all of creation, yet we defer to something more animalistic that's all too common in all of creation. And that primal, animalistic side of us is more often than not the 'primary' side of us. We know it to be inferior, but it's easily reachable. It's easier to believe that the whole of ourselves is made up of this primal part because to master it, force it into submission, bend it to our will and bring it into full obedience requires assets that we don't view ourselves as possessing. We are not good enough to be good enough. We will fall victim to our baser self rather than rise to a higher self that we don't believe exists. And that's a problem because we are better than this.

Yet, the good within us is stirred by challenges such as this. That 'good' within us is aroused by an anger that something as vehemently attacking as this would dare raise its head and casually stroll the concourses of our lives without being confronted. For the good within us, there is an ever-increasing yearning to crush its head and sweep it from our lives by proving it wrong. Bad incites good. Bad ignites good. Bad arouses good from slumber and sends it roaring into our lives. And if we unleash the great good within us, the bad doesn't stand a chance because we truly are better than this.

The Thought of Not Thinking
It seems that we're relatively slow to think and dreadfully quick to react. We're sluggish to methodically strategize our actions, while we're reflexively quick to strike out in some sort of impulsive reaction. We reflexively react to the crisis of the moment not realizing that such reactions can unnecessarily press the crisis into a future within which it does not belong. Rather than draw upon the expanse of our intellect and the depth of our wisdom, particularly in the difficult times, we too often grab the closest thing to us and start swinging. The fact of the matter is that we are better than this.

Because we do, we become defined by our actions. We believe that the nature of our choices and the legacy of our exploits tell us who we are, when in fact they tell us who we've chosen to be.

Others have said that we are an abysmal 'nothing' who can't leverage anything good or bad because we have nothing to leverage. Therefore, our actions become an entirely reflexive and incessantly gyrating manifestation of the nothing from which they arose. In fact, we are better than this.

Typically who we've chosen to be is our response to the power of fear reining in the best of ourselves so that what's left to run wild is the worst of ourselves. The belief that there's nothing better within us leaves the best of us gagged, bound and silenced in an oblivion of seeming nonexistence. And who we've chosen to be plays itself out enough times that we become convinced that this is who we are when in fact, we are better than this.

Falling to this lesser self, we're too often not prudent and anything but judicious. We've too easily abandoned our intellectual capabilities and we react in less than thoughtful ways. And when we do that long enough, we tend to forget that we have the ability to be and to act in ways that are far above what we're being, and far more judicious than how we're acting. We're slowly led to believe that we're more primal than anything else, and that a keen discernment and a prudent approach is either beyond us, or that it 'takes too much work' to get there. We eventually believe that this lesser self is the entirely of ourselves. We believe a message reinforced by our actions that is not reflective of our abilities. We are, in fact, better than this.

Is It Beyond Us?

Too often we use the whole mentality that something's beyond us as an excuse to avoid using what's actually within us. We don't want to be all that accountable, or we're not really all that interested in stepping up, or we don't want to extend ourselves, or a million other excuses for the inexcusable attitudes of mediocrity and apathy. We don't want to believe that we have sufficient acumen to be responsible because then we would need to be responsible when we'd prefer to leave that to someone who is more responsible. "We could never do that," we incessantly tell ourselves as a means of lulling ourselves into some sort of stale complacency. "We don't have it within us," we whisper to ourselves so that we don't have to display it outside of us. And in doing so, we penalize our spirits, forfeit our abilities and levy a heavy fine on our capabilities. We are better than this even though we may be convinced otherwise.

Writing Bad Narratives

The only things that are beyond us are the things that we tell ourselves are beyond us. We are our own worst narrator. We are storytellers of the most spellbinding sort. However, what gets bound in the binding is the richness of the tale regarding who we actually are. We cast ourselves as the villain of our own script, or the failure of our own storyline or the lost cause that's not a cause at all.

As such, we are not the reality of the narrative even though we penned it. Rather, it's the depth to which we chose to believe these errant narratives. And in whatever manner we choose to believe them, we must be careful to understand the rationale for that belief. The rationale is typically one of surrender to the fear that we are the terrible person that we think we are. The script is one of surrender. Or maybe we're more than what we think we are, but the size of who we might be is frightening enough to keep us from writing that into any kind of narrative. Bad narratives are the stuff of everything that we are not, for we are better than this.

Is It Too Much Work?
The fact that acting with wisdom, prudence and discretion takes some time and requires a bit of energy is quite often something less than appealing. To act wisely and thoughtfully means that we purposefully rally our intellectual resources, apply those resources in order to carefully ascertain the situation, make judicious decisions based on our observations and then engage the situation with wisdom, balance and discernment.

That all takes time and energy, and often it takes a lot of it. Too often we're not really all that interested in expending that kind of time and energy because we'd much prefer to speedily dispense with whatever we're facing, or all we're really interested in is driving an agenda and nothing more. In reality, we probably want to get on to something that's much more fun and much less demanding, or we want simply want to run as far away as humanly possible. So we do what we have to do to simply get it done. And such a slipshod approach has slipshod outcomes that leave us slipping all over the place. Despite the fact that such behaviors ardently reinforce our low self-esteem, we are better than this.

It's Everywhere
Sadly, these behaviors aren't exclusive to us. In fact, they seem to be becoming a whole lot more prevalent in our culture these days. We watch individuals at all levels in all kinds of roles and in an endless variety of occupations doing the very same thing. Frequently we have an expectation that individuals in certain roles should be acting wisely, thoughtfully and with an astute judiciousness. To us, it's clear that people in certain positions of authority or in critical situations should be acting with a keen degree of prudence and reacting with an unbiased discretion. Yet, often they don't. And so we see this malaise and indifference populating the actions and behaviors of people everywhere. In time, we devolve into the assumption that it's just the way it is. This is life. Any other expectations are magical at best and to be disappointed at worst. And over time, we tragically lose the understanding that we are better

than this.

Reclamation

We are better than this. We are better than how we behave. We are better than the ways in which we act. We are better than what our decisions would suggest and what our actions would portray. We are better than the image that we have projected into the world around us, and the reflection of ourselves that we see within. We are better than the narratives we have penned and we are superior to the assassinations of self that we've penned into them. We are better than our failures and deeper than our fears. We are better than the reach of our imaginations because we are created by a God who is beyond the reach of our understanding. We are better than this!

I would rather pointedly and somewhat adamantly suggest that it's time to reclaim the fact that we are better than this. It's time to step up and refuse to be less than what we are. And in reclaiming the fact that we are better than this, it's high time that we not only believe it but deliberately act upon it. It's time that we get past the errant idea that it's 'beyond us' and that it takes 'too much work' to do it. It's time that we step into the mindboggling expanse of who we were created to be, recognize the enormity of what that is, and live it out with a stubborn intensity and intentionality. It's time to wake up and realize that we are better than this even though everything might scream that we are worse than this.

144

How's it Done?

As with any great things in life, simple answers are simply insufficient. But let me propose a place to begin:

First, I think that we need to recognize the foundational reality that we are more than what we've come to believe ourselves to be. Change begins with this simple, but critical realization. We might not necessarily know exactly what that is, or exactly what that means, or exactly what that looks like, but it's developing the fundamental recognition that we are 'more.' That recognition creates the awareness of a space that's largely uninhabited, but a space that's entirely available to us. It begins the process of breaking down the walls that we've created around us that have come to define the extent of us. It helps us understand that the majority of who we are lies outside of the walls that have come to define who we are. That reality fosters a compelling willingness to move up and move out from wherever it is that we are because we've recognized that there's an endless place to actually do that.

Second, it's about intentionally being better and deliberately doing better. It's about recognizing the limitations that we've habitually embraced, confronting those limitations when they pop up and asking ourselves how we can take one step beyond them this time around. It's refusing to fall prey to the old messages by speaking a new truth into them. It's about identifying that this is how far we'd typically take something, and then purposefully taking it one step further, or two steps if we're sufficiently daring. It's about persistence and purposefulness in the pursuit of something better.

Third, once we've taken a step further, it's about recognizing that it actually worked because it typically does. It's about reinforcing the fact that we actually felt pretty good about it because we typically do. It's about pondering the fact that we went where we typically don't go and in going there it went really well, because it typically will. It's understanding that typically nothing bad happens and that as wildly unbelievable as it might seem, it was the same for us. It's accepting that we're not as 'typical' as we believed ourselves to be and that the fact of the matter is we're anything but typical. And finally, it's about feeling that we're better than what we've historically chosen to be because we are, and now we're actually experiencing it!

Fourth, it's living all of this out right in front of the very people that we encounter every single day. 'We are better than this,' and we want that reality to become rampantly contagious to everyone that we meet. We want people to wonder what happened, how it happened, and how it can happen for them. We want to create this infectious influenza that causes people to step up, step out, and step into

Craig D. Lounsbrough

of the belief that they are better than this for the simple reason that they are. And as we see that emerge in the lives of others it becomes increasingly convincing that it is, in fact, happening in our lives.

We Are Better Than This
We are better than this.' It may be that we are living in a time in history where that message and that reality needs to be broadcast with all the intensity and every bit of emotion that we can muster. We need to proclaim this reality with a voice, an intensity and a conviction unparalleled. We appear to live in times that beg each of us to passionately live out of the conviction that 'we are better than this' so that this world becomes better than what it is. And we need to live it out so that we might take our low self-esteem and start drowning it out.

And in doing so, we need to rally those around us those who embrace and live out this same conviction. We need to become an immovable mass that gains an unstoppable momentum of irrepressible change. Indeed, if we respond to this reality we can change the world because the indisputable truth is that 'we are better than this' which will make the world that we live in better than what it is. And a crusade of this sort begins with the sort of people that are just like you and me.

The Hard Questions:
1. Take a moment, sit down and write out at least

twenty positive characteristics that you possess.

2. Take that list and put it somewhere where you will see it every day. Read it to yourself once in the morning when you get up, and once at night before you go to bed.

3. Pick one characteristic each day that you will focus on, work to exhibit, and purposefully manifest throughout the day.

Chapter 11
A Bigger Person
Reclaiming the Majesty of Our Humanity

"So God created mankind in his own image, in the image of God he created them; male and female he created them."
- Genesis 1:27 (NIV)

"Let no man pull you low enough to hate him."
- Martin Luther King

The majesty of our humanity and the capabilities laid out within us are nothing short of marvelous; so much so that we are barely cognizant of it. That in and of itself may be why we don't recognize them and therefore don't believe that they exist. All of us run deep with untapped potential that is rustling just under the surface of our lives waiting to be unleashed. There is something of an innate greatness within us that seems to exceed the reach of our ability to believe in until we forcefully work to do so. We are rich with possibility and formidably equipped to tease the cusp of the impossible and to overcome it.

The essence of our being is immense beyond words and the breadth of it eclipses any syntax to frame it. The potential inside of us lays outside of our ability to explain it. We are greater than the definitions that we would craft to define ourselves or the rubrics that we would construct to lend ourselves identifiable parameters. Subsequently, if we can't explain something or reign it in by the application of a definition we question the reality of it because we can't frame it with words or harness it with intellect. If we can't do either of those, whatever we thought ourselves to be must not be.

We are bigger than ourselves, and therefore most of who we are we never see. We never see it because we don't look. And we don't look because we too often believe that there's nothing to look for. And if perchance we do look (whether purposefully or by accident) too often we can't describe the vastness of it or frame it in a manner that makes it manageable. Therefore, we turn our attention to the demands of lesser things and we plod on in the valley of lesser things, finding ourselves shaped by our habitation in the dullness of such valleys.

Intricate in Design
Despite the incomprehensible complexity of our being or our inability to grasp it, the entirety of this essence is seamlessly consolidated and ingeniously joined so that the full measure of it might be released without any of it wasted or missed in the releasing. Indeed it's complex, but it's ingenious in its complexity. It's perfectly joined and precisely unified. It might be massive in scope to the point that we may not understand it nor grasp the breathtaking potency of it, but it is joined together without our

need to join it together. It works in synch with the whole of itself leaving nothing out of the process.

We would be wise to understand that who we are will work itself out if we simply exercise a degree of faith in it, relinquish our need to control it, move away from the desire to exercise it for selfish gain and surrender our limited habitats for the unexplored habitats that lie beyond our walls of fear. All of the parts are there and they are joined in perfect synchronization so as to take on the journeys that we thought to be impossible to take on. We hold within ourselves more than we realize. We contain the ingredients for achieving the impossible.

Created to Stand Above

We are crafted to enhance all that exists around us and to make everything immeasurably more than what is. We are not made to simply maintain our existence, for that would marginalize the scope of our abilities in the service of something terribly menial. Such an endeavor is an illusion born of the belief that 'status quo' is possible in a world that is forever in motion. Maintenance is the refuge of the frightened. It is a place of surrender. It is the creation of some sort of minimally habitable hovel where we live out sequestered lives that only reinforce this very sequestered sense of who we are and what we're capable of. As such, such a place is never a place of maintenance. Rather, it is a place of deterioration and perpetual demise.

Rather, we are marvelous in ways so grand that such marvel escapes us even though it resides right within each of us. That is the oddity of it all. Our grandness is not speculation nor fanciful theory. Our potential is not something of muse, as we might presume it to be since we tend to see so little of it. It's not some hollow ideal that is more the trappings of some imaginative author who spins such ideas because they don't have the courage to face the realities of who or what we really are. This is not about some feeble attempt to bolster our belief in ourselves as we watch the worst of ourselves create a world that we're turning into the worst of itself. It's not some idea that warms us up to the bad that we see in ourselves so that we can live with ourselves. This potential is real. Very real. It may visit us rarely as it is much easier to access the lesser side of ourselves. But it's real, and it's always waiting.

Misplacing Majesty - Playground Feuds and Turf Wars

We have misplaced the majesty of our humanity in the lesser battles that we readily (and rather ignorantly) join. We cast ourselves as heroes selflessly battling for the soul of a community, a family or a nation when in fact we are engaged in playgrounds feuds of no greater importance than those played out on elementary playgrounds. We lay claim to some turf, which is less about what the turf might actually be and more about the fact that it's turf (whatever it might be). We see ourselves on some colossal pilgrimage born of calling or destiny or the rallying of the masses against some great evil, however we have justified it.

It must be pointed out that at times the pilgrimages are in fact colossal and of significant importance. Sometimes they are the entirely pristine call of God pressing us out into a world to bring something of inestimable value to that world. Sometimes these endeavors are pure beyond imagination and glorious beyond comprehension. Sometimes they are 'right' in a way that makes right magnificent.

But too many times what's colossal is the appetite of our egos verses the worthiness of the venture. Or the voice of the culture that demands obedient adherence to some trend or ideal lest that culture cast us aside and brand us as ignorant and culturally incompatible. It might be competition for a job, or competition with a neighbor, or competition with ourselves or competition with competition. For whatever reason, too often we engage in these dirty little mongering turf wars that are more the stuff of mudslinging than anything that might raise up humanity or change the course of history itself.

We wallow in the bane of blustering banter and then we gorge it fat on reckless arguments whose goal is to win, with us long having forgotten what exactly it is that we're trying to win. Everything becomes a tit-for-tat circus of push and shove that might be equated to two toddlers fighting over a toy that neither of them really wants in the first place. The focus becomes on finding some weakness, some point of hidden vulnerability, some crack in the proverbial armor that we can exploit in the pursuit of pursuing. We want to posture ourselves as some sort of valiant and sturdy victor, and if perchance we fall to the throes of defeat we then position ourselves as the victim whose defeat clearly illustrates the impenetrable validity of their cause. And in the depravity and insanity of all of this we have misplaced the majesty of our humanity and we have wholly abandoned our calling.

Often the feud is with ourselves. These fear-mongering turf wars happen inside of ourselves. They're born of a gritty self-hatred wherein we are seeking the destruction of self because we are unable to see the value of self. As Pogo once said, "We have met the enemy and he is us." We are not a friend to ourselves. In fact, most times we are not even a congenial acquaintance. Rather, we are a foe. We are an adversary. We are all that is worthy of hatred and disgust. I would suggest that the majority of the battles that we fight are with ourselves, against ourselves and out of hatred for ourselves. And who we are devolves into the smallness of these internal battles. Who we are is compromised in the battle of lesser things and we fall to becoming a lesser person.

Evolution of Our Identity

Despite notions to the contrary, we do not become identified by the nature of the battles that we're fighting. Rather, we become identified by the fact that we're fighting them. We are those conniving people on some rant either outlandishly ubiquitous or stealthy and silent. We've exchanged some meaningless turf war or circular entanglement for everything else so that there seems to be nothing else. Our sense of self becomes consumed by such reckless endeavors and we become the sum total of these actions. We then decry our filthiness and our reckless mentality, yet we continue to engage in these behaviors and we become increasingly identified by them in the engagements.

Any sense of majesty that would call us to a higher road is forgotten. As we continue to be immersed in these behaviors over time, any such sense of majesty is gradually eaten away at the edges and eventually it's deemed not to exist at all. We either believe that we never possessed such majesty, or we did but we effectively destroyed it beyond redemption in these dirty little turf wars. So we slowly plummet into some sense of free-falling self-degradation and escalating personal disappointment. And our self-esteem slowly, or sometimes not so slowly perishes.

Part of the appealing nature of these turf wars and meaningless entanglements rest in the fact that they have granted us a sorely needed sense of identity and value. They impart unto us a definitive and identifiable sense of personhood as we become identified as someone engaged in a grand pursuit of whatever it is that we're pursing, or whatever it is we're trying to destroy. We have purpose. We have a cause to rally around, or we have created a cause to rally around. Our lives have subsequently been imparted with meaning. We are finally somebody because we finally stand for something, even if the standing is something more akin to crawling. Therefore, the nature of the battles becomes secondary to the fact that we've finally got one that grants us an identity.

Have we chosen the right things to stand for out of the desperate need to stand for something? Are we really standing, or in some sense are we really thrashing about in a decadent endeavor aimed at our own destruction? Is the battle a worthy battle, or did we choose it more to destroy something and less to win something? And if that's the case, how often is that 'thing' ourselves? Are these battles ultimately less about the battle and more about justifying the destruction of ourselves by rationalizing the rightness of the battle? Such an action is not as improbable as it might sound. And if we are engaged in battles of this sort, our self-esteem is certain to suffer.

To Reclaim Our Majesty

Might it be time to be accountable to who we've become so that we can make ourselves accountable to what we can be? Are we willing to divest ourselves of all the lesser things that we have elevated as greater things and engage in both a pointed and painful evaluation of who we've become? Are we willing to abandon ourselves to what is right by abandoning all that is wrong, even if we have to abandon this sorely needed sense of self in the process? Can we see that the battle might be the way that we are destroying ourselves by believing that we're saving something else? And can we let that go?

Are we sufficiently prudent and thoughtful to realize that what we've engaged in and committed ourselves to might, in fact, be the very thing that gave us an identity but destroyed our self-esteem at the very same time? Are we willing to make the cause that which is right rather than that which is expedient or popular? For in the end, the greatest cause is not the cause, but the God who calls us to the cause. And any calling that He extends will always build our self-esteem and bolster our sense of self.

Honest Assessment as Moving Forward

Once we've performed that bit of self-scrutiny, are we brave enough to look at the damage that we're incurred in the becoming? Can we relinquish our claim to whatever bit of turf we've claimed and lay our playground feuds to rest in deference to a cause far greater than the tiny space that we occupy? Can we shake ourselves out of ourselves sufficiently to wake up to the far greater things that lay 'round about us? Can we begin to see others less as enemies and more as people whose differing views may inform our own? Can we do the same for ourselves? At what point will we understand that partnership and camaraderie must be preserved even when differences of beliefs or opinions would do their level best to blast us into warring camps? When will we forfeit what we've become in order to become something so vastly superior to what we've become?

More than that, can we come to terms with ourselves? Can we find peace with us? As we pointed out, more often than not we are the enemy. We are the thing that ignited this crusade that we've launched against ourselves. We fight others as an extension of the battle that we are waging within ourselves. The enemy out there is often an unwitting victim of the enemy 'in here.' Therefore, can we forgive ourselves? Can we see the value of ourselves and out of that find some thin shred of love for ourselves? Can we recognize that the battle against self is a perpetual civil war of stalled engagements where both sides are destined to lose? Can we be bigger than what we've chosen to be?

The Shift
It's not that such a shift is impossible (despite the fact that the behaviors exhibited in our world might

suggest otherwise). But in the face of the reckless insanity all around us and within us, will we dare to dare? Will we raise ourselves up to embrace the fullness of our humanity? Will we cast off the scourge of selfish agendas and the saber-rattling born of insatiable egos and internal battles? Will we be what we've chosen not to be at whatever cost we might pay to do so, recognizing that the cost of not doing so is far, far greater? Will we shed all that we've become to become all that we can be? In essence, will we reclaim the majesty of our humanity as it was created and tenderly fashioned to be instead of turning it against ourselves and everyone else?

And in answering this myriad array of questions, do we realize that this is about reclaiming all that is good so that we might become all that is great? That we will choose the higher road as a means of reclaiming our majesty, rather than falling to the depths to claim some sense of identity that has altogether forgotten what majesty is? And it is in this painful and exacting self-examination that we will reawaken a greater sense of self that we have otherwise forsaken. We will begin to both see and understand the inherent majesty that God has intimately woven within us. And in seeing that, how can we not have a restored and reignited self-esteem?

I Believe

I am utterly confident in our ability to do all of those things. But to do so, we must recognize what we've done 'wrong' so that what we should do 'right' becomes sharply apparent. As this dichotomy becomes increasingly apparent and the distinctions sharpen, the 'good' within us will be stirred and challenged by the 'bad' all around us. But it's the recognition of the 'bad' and calling it out for what it is instead of dressing it up in something that's it's not. It's realizing that the call of so many things around us are the call of something other than our inherent majesty, for that majesty silently calls us to something bigger that intimidates the call of all of things lesser. And I believe that we can heed that higher call. More than that, I believe that we can live by it.

I have great hope in humanity. Because we choose lesser things does not mean that we are lesser people. Because we've succumbed to the lie of low self-esteems doesn't mean that we are what they say we are. It means that we have settled for mediocrity, or we fear running against the grain of a culture sliding sideways, or we've been schooled in lesser things and we're simply being the obedient student, or we don't see within ourselves any kind of place where majesty might take up the residence it never left.

But under the unappealing layers there rests

something of grandeur that the layers will never kill. There is something of God in each of us that lies dormant. It stirs on occasion. It calls out if we push aside the boisterous noise of a culture relentlessly pounding out its agendas in brash tones and edgy verbiage. It tenderly pricks our conscience when we lash out at others because we're lashing out at ourselves, and it tells us that neither are deserving of what we are doing to both. It tells us that we are bigger than what we've become.

That majesty is there. It's breathing. It's hoping for its moment. It's poised to leap to the forefront of everything that we are. It's ours for the taking because it is ours by design. It's more of who we are than everything that the culture would say that we are, or our self-esteem would declare. And once we awaken ourselves to these realities, the impossible becomes possible, every longing finds its deepest needs met and our self-esteem will spring to abundant life.

Hope in God
I have even greater hope in the God that bestowed us with abilities that in fact mirrored His own. That in and of itself is astounding. This God did not cut corners or create out of compromise. He did not craft us in a hurried and harried fashion for He had all of eternity to do the crafting. There were no limits to the vast resources available to Him when He crafted us out of the genius of His infinite creativity.

The Self That I Long to Believe In

We were designed from the massive vault of eternity past and endowed with ample resources to live into and through eternity future. The Master Craftsman pronounced us as "very good," which means we possess a great good. And it is in this Great God that we can be assured of our own greatness.

For these reasons, I have a pervading and insatiable hope. Though some might say so, I do not believe that kind of hope to be misplaced. I do not believe it to be idealistic or the misplaced muse of someone who fears embracing the realities of the horrors that we can most certainly perpetrate. This is not a product of a fatiguing heart that has been continually pummeled by the nature of the news or the climate of the culture. It's not because it rests in a God Who supersedes every shred of everything that would shred us.

I believe in us: in you and me. I believe that we have not done well, but I believe we can yet do very well. I believe that we have made horrible mistakes, but I believe that we can do great good. I believe in something better. I believe that we can join together in a mutual assault on the mounting challenges in our world instead of engaging in mounting assaults on each other and on ourselves. I believe. And I hope that every one of us might join me in that belief. And in that joining might we rigorously inventory how we can be different. And then let us go and begin the process of making things different. Let us reclaim the majesty of our humanity in the care of humanity both without and within. And in that reclamation, let's reclaim our self-esteem and begin to see ourselves as majestic as God sees us.

The Hard Questions:

1. What are the turf wars and various battles that you've chosen to engage in?
2. Why did you choose these and what have they done for you?
3. Which of these are the lesser things that you need to rid yourself of?

Chapter 12
Knock Me Down
The Art of Getting Up

"Have I not commanded you? Be strong and courageous. Do not be afraid; do not be discouraged, for the LORD your God will be with you wherever you go."
- Joshua 1:9 (NIV)

"Everyone falls down. Getting back up is how you learn how to walk."
- Walt Disney

The issue in life is not how many times we get knocked down, although we're pretty well convinced that it's the major issue when we're lying flat on our backs staring up at the sky of defeat once again. Nonetheless, the issue in life is not how many times we get knocked down. The pain of the fall and the disappointment of being on a piece of ground that have become all too familiar cause us to focus on the fact that, yet again, we got knocked down. But that's not the issue.

We can focus on why we got knocked down, how many times we've gotten knocked down before, or how often we've gotten knocked down in the same place for the same reasons. We can ponder what we did, what we didn't do and the series of rather spurious decisions that led us to the fall. We can think about the fact that we were still 'smarting' from the last time that we got knocked down, and here we are on the ground yet again not even fully recovered from the last fall. And while our focus is centered on how many times we've gotten knocked down, the fact that we're staring at the sky while laying prostrate on the ground is not the issue...at all. And if we are to build our self-esteem, it cannot be our focus.

The Imperative Nature of Getting Back Up

The issue in life is how many times we get back up. That sounds rather trite and a bit too obvious to be of much value. But it only seems to be of marginal value because we've yet to understand the imperative nature of getting back up and the impetus of character that's involved in such a seemingly simple action. Given the statement that's made in such an action as well as the repercussions that will follow, getting back up is far more than just getting back up.

What Getting Back Up Acknowledges

Getting back up boldly and sometimes humbly acknowledges that we got knocked down in the first place. It is an acceptance of a less than successful and reinforcing event that we need to accept if we are to do anything about it. Getting back up also forces us to face all of the dynamics that contributed to that fall, most of which are likely the less than wise or flattering decisions that led us here and laid us flat.

It's a transparent and frank accountability of our role in getting knocked down, for if we place blame for the position that we're in we'll find ourselves frequently visiting that place.

Getting back up is a clear and uncompromising statement that we are willing to face what knocked us down. In all probability, whatever knocked us down still must be contended with. It's highly likely that it remains a challenge or an adversary or an obstacle. Therefore, getting back up will obviously involve the effort to get back up. However, it also includes the additional expenditure of energy that will be involved in a battle that is certain to be resumed because we got back up.

Additionally, whatever knocked us down has often positioned itself to keep us down. In most instances, getting knocked down was only part of a larger strategy to keep us down and therefore render us perpetually impotent. Getting knocked down is often the first action in a prolonged action designed to keep us down. Therefore, getting back up will likely be met with resistance to keep us down so that knocking us down again will be unnecessary.

The Cost of Not Getting Back Up
It's not all that difficult to figure out that if the amount of times we get up is just one less than the amount of times that we've been knocked down, then we're spending our lives lying down. Life will

knock us down...guaranteed. And it will do it more than once. That's guaranteed as well. Whether it simply causes us to stagger as we reel from its variant blows, or it hits us with enough blunt force to drop us to our knees, or if it rams with us with an impact that levels us and lays us flat on our backs. In whatever way it happens, life will knock us down. And rather than let our self-esteems take a hit, we must continually remind ourselves that life works this way. It's a sign that we're living it, not necessarily a sign that it's leveling us.

As we noted, life often works to keep us down. Therefore, there's the action that knocks us down, followed by the continued action of keeping us down. Whether that's life hitting us so brutally hard that the effects will be sustained for some time, thereby keeping us down. Or, if it's the elongated nature of the circumstances that maintain a sustained pressure upon us. Or, whether it's life hitting us repeatedly in the same place in the same way so that the repetition makes us increasingly tentative about ever getting up again. In whatever way that it happens, life not only wants us down, but it wants us to stay down. And if we do, our self-esteem will rot in the laying.

Knocked Down as a Correlation to Our Worth

Sometimes we assume that being knocked down is in correlation to our worth. That life has targeted us due to some glaring deficit or screaming inadequacy or blatant weakness. That life has chosen to beat us up as some arrogantly roaming bully picking on a pathetically weak person who is unable to defend themselves. There's a cost in living out our lives in the basement of the social hierarchy. And since our low self-esteem has prompted us to take up residency in that place, we pay the price others impose on us who've recognized that as our habitation. We become labeled as personally disadvantaged people who are easy targets for those who can't resolve their own issues except to dump them on others. Or at least that's how we see it. And from this vantage point, our self-esteem can only be continually pummeled.

What Getting Knocked Down Tells Us
But I think that there's an entirely different way to look at it. I think that getting knocked down might actually tell us how we're living life. In a sense, figuring out how robustly we're living life, or not living life, is really rather rudimentary. Although it might seem a tad bit simplistic, all we have to do is look at the number of times we get knocked down. The fact is the number of times that we're knocked flat is in direct correlation to how aggressively we're pressing into this thing that we call life. If we're running headlong into life, life is going to run headlong into us. If we refuse the petty boundaries that we sheepishly place around us and mindfully push past those boundaries, life will push back. It's

in the momentum of moving forward that life works to press us backward.

And in the impending running, and pushing, and colliding that's a part of it all, we will get knocked down. It's inevitable. But it's also reinforcing. It evidences that we are not standing still nor sitting down. We are up and running, or at least walking. So, getting knocked down might be less related to our self of worthlessness and more about the fact that we're actually trying to go somewhere.

So if we're not getting knocked down, it's likely because we're not going anywhere to get knocked down. And that could very well indicate a passively sedentary and pathetically mediocre life. The choice in life is whether we're going to take our hits because we've decided to move forward, or we've determined to play it safe by staying in pretty much the same place. How many times we get knocked down is in direct correlation to how aggressively we're running out into life. And so, it might be worthwhile to do the math and determine how many times we've been knocked down because that suggests the degree to which we are attempting to move forward.

The Growth in Getting Knocked Down

We might also consider the fact that the greatest lessons come in the greatest falls. There is the actual act of falling, and then there is the act of paying attention to nothing else other than the fact that we fell down. Yet, the far greater part is what we can learn in the fall. It's not that we got knocked down. It's the lessons that are available to us when we get knocked down. It's dissecting all the variant elements of the fall, discerning their individual roles in the fall, understanding their corporate effects in making the fall happen, and then taking those lessons and applying them. The harder the fall, the greater the lessons. The more frequent the falls, the greater the opportunities.

In each fall we are handed something that is unlike any other fall. No individual fall is exactly the same as the last one. Therefore, there are fresh insights every time. We can grow strong. We can learn. We can grow wise. We can develop depth. We can cultivate a penetrating discernment and sharpen our vision to a razor focus. We can profoundly enhance our understanding of both ourselves and life. So while we are apt to allow each fall to further rip our self-esteem to pieces, we miss the nearly unimaginable opportunities in each fall. And it is those opportunities that are generously embedded with the very resources that can work against our low self-esteem in ways that few things can.

Being knocked down strengthens our ability to get up. Being knocked down deepens our resolve to work against whatever is trying to keep us down.

Being knocked down enlivens our appreciation of what it is to stand up. Being knocked down widens our empathy for others who've been knocked down. Looking up from the place that we've been knocked down to grants us a unique perspective that we don't have when we're standing up. Looking up is what incites us to rise up beyond just standing up. These perspectives come with unfathomable insight and lessons rich beyond our understanding. Indeed, they are the very lessons that, when brought to bear upon and pressed against our low self-esteem can utterly transform that self-esteem.

What Keeps Us Down

The Dance of Avoidance

If we look around us, there's a whole lot of people doing a whole lot of dancing, and we're often part of that crowd. The intent of this dance is to skirt around whatever the things are that are likely to knock us down. It's the classic 'bob and weave' where we anxiously look ahead and squint at the horizon in front of us in order to discern what's coming at us from whatever distance it's coming from. And if whatever's coming at us appears powerful enough to drop us to our knees, or if it's moving fast enough to lay us flat on our backs, we dance around it.

In reality, there's nothing inherently wrong about being smart about life and proceeding with some degree of wisdom and caution. A little dancing in the right place at the right times for the right reasons certainly has value. Yet, too often this dancing is not about effective navigation as much as it's about all-out avoidance. Although we don't think about it a whole lot, the energy and momentum expended in the dance sacrifices forward momentum. To waste energy in the effort to 'avoid' something is to trade away our future to protect ourselves in the present. And being stuck in such a fashion can be the death knell to our self-esteem.

We end up dancing for sure, but as we noted, most often we're doing nothing more than dancing in place because the dance doesn't leave us with any leftover energy to propel us forward. And we think that because life hasn't been knocking us down, the dancing that we're doing is obviously quite shrewd and very successful and possibly rather ingenious. We think ourselves to be pretty clever and we figure that we've got life pretty much figured out because we haven't been knocked down.

What we miss is that we're not getting knocked down because we're not moving forward sufficiently to have anything knock us down. There's no momentum. We're just dancing in place. We're holding the fort, digging in, holing up and parking it in whatever place that we're parking it in. We'd be wise to recognize the fact that when life knocks us down, our avoidance will keep us down.

Denial – Keeping Us Down

And then there's the choice of living in denial that we're quite often living in the denial of. When life causes us to stagger as we reel from its variant blows, or when it hits us with enough blunt force to drop us to our knees, or when it collides with us with an impact that levels us and lays us flat on our backs, we're often in denial that any of that's happened at all. And we can become so adept at denial that we often don't even realize that anything's really happening because our denial has thoroughly convinced us that what's happening is not. Because that's the case, we can be down for the count and think that we're up for the challenge. We can find ourselves dead in our tracks and think that we're making tracks.

All of this is compounded by the fact that denial can make us think that we're in the game when we're actually somewhere on some distant sideline so far removed from the game that we're not even certain what or where the game is anymore. We can believe that we're out there pressing into this thing that we call life when the only thing that we're pressing into is the armchair that we've parked ourselves in. We can be utterly convinced that we're trekking up the road when we're not leaving a single track behind us. When life knocks us down, our denial will keep us down. And that will keep our self-esteem down as well.

Hit Me – Refusing to Stay Down

If life's not hitting us, it's because we're not hitting life. If life isn't pushing us, then it's obvious we're not pushing it. The calm in the storm might be due to the fact that we've not even entered the storm. The road before us might be austere, broad and placid only because we've intentionally run from any road of any sort that had any hint of challenge even remotely associated with it. The sun might be raining golden shafts of pristine light on our lives only because we've circumvented anything that's even marginally cloudy or overcast. Even for those of us who relentlessly forge ahead, we will have calm days as that is the natural ebb and flow of life. But calm for too long begs the question of whether we're in an all-out pursuit of life, or we're all out of the pursuit of life.

I want to press into life, and I want to do that relentlessly. When my life is over, I want to make absolutely certain that what I've left behind me is immeasurably greater than what I've left in front of me. I want the finish line of my race to be as far from the starting line as I can possibly get it. I don't want to end my life staring up some long road that lies in front of me that should lie behind me instead. If I let that happen, I have let my self-esteem get the better of me which will only serve to get the better of it.

And to end up somewhere near the end of that kind of road will mean that I'm going to get hit

174

along the way. I'm not all that interested in inviting the blows that life will wield, and I have no intent of egging life on. But I'm not going to run from those blows either. And I think that the sign of a purposeful life lived with fixed intention is the recognition that it's going to get hit, and that it possesses the willingness to have that happen. It also possesses the understanding that getting hit is not a commentary on life beating me up because I'm easy to beat up. It's beating me up because I'm determined enough to walk headlong into it.

And so I'd rather be hit because that means I'm headed somewhere versus being lost in the 'nowhere' that dancing and denial will plant me. It means that I didn't allow a poor self-image to keep me laying prostrate in the dirt and that instead I chose to press against whatever decided to press against me. And when I gain that perspective through the trials that the forward movement is certain to bring, my self-esteem grows and my confidence begins to flourish.

Hit Me – Getting Up

When I'm hit, I'm going to get up. I'm going to get up, because to not get up is to end the journey of my life right in the exact place where I got knocked down. To not get up is to say that whatever knocked me down is bigger than my ability to get back up. To not get up is to say that life has the ability to beat me decades before the grave brings it all to a close, leaving me to spend those decades doing nothing more than waiting for death to show up. To not get up is to say that my goal is not worth the price of getting to that goal. To not get back up is to declare defeat as my lot in life, and to embrace surrender as the solution. And so, I refuse not to get back up.

We all get hit, and we all get knocked down. That's part of the journey of this thing that we call life. It's inevitable. We can get caught up in the fact that getting knocked down was unfair, unjust, that it was due to another person's incompetence or it was a product of circumstances that we had no part in at all. We can complain and whine and have a full-blown tantrum about all the reasons why we find ourselves flat on our backs. But none of that gets us up when we're down. None of that puts us on our feet.

The only thing that gets us up is the conviction that we're not going to stay down regardless of what put us down, or what might put us down the next time. It's a commitment to always being on our feet and to getting back on our feet should we find ourselves somewhere else other than our feet. It embraces a firm sense of duty and a deeply embedded feeling of obligation that we simply cannot and will not surrender this gift that we call life to slavish mediocrity or the bane of fear.

We need to get up because not doing so is a

life squandered and an opportunity wasted. We need to get up because we don't want to find ourselves at the end of our lives still at the beginning of the road of our lives. We need to get up because anything less is less than what we can live with. We need to get up as a clear and sustained declaration that we are superior to the lies that our low self-esteem has spoken into us for most of our lives. The issue in life is not how many times we get knocked down. The issue in life is how many times we get back up and how many times we feed a languishing self-esteem because we did. So, let's get up and let's get going.

The Hard Questions:
1. When was the last time that you got knocked down? Think through the event.
2. Did you get back up? If so, how did you do that. If not, what you do plan on doing to get up?
3. What is the plan the next time you get knocked down?

Chapter 13
My Imagination
The Limits of My Mind

"Do you see a someone skilled in their work? They will serve before kings; they will not serve before officials of low rank."
- Proverbs 22:29 (NIV)

"The man who has no imagination has no wings."
- Muhammad Ali

Some of us have very vivid imaginations. We can effortlessly conjure up an endless litany of wildly creative concepts, mind-bending visions, and far-reaching theories that can eclipse the very imagination from which they were birthed. We can be ingenious beyond the limits of our own ingenuity. We can poke at the impossible and see if it's as impossible as it would lead us to believe. We can take the bland raw materials that lay scattered around us and craft wonderfully vivid visions that transform everything around us. Whatever the case, some of us can be wildly creative without a whole lot of substance to use in the creating. At times we find our own creations electrifying, but we can also find them a little baffling as we're not certain how we came up with them or exactly what to do with them now that we've come up with them.

Then there are others of us whose ingenuity

178

and imagination are a bit more concrete. There are those of us who are more firmly grounded in the realities that we see around us. Our musings are more dictated by taking handfuls, or possibly bucketfuls of the raw stuff of life that we journey through and molding that coarse material with a sprinkling of ingenuity, a dollop of creativity and a dash of passion, which results in something rather creative, but wholly practical. We're more strategic and we tend toward refined calculations. There's a transparently clean, tight and well-defined course of action that's embarked upon through a deliberate series of steps, rather than running wholesale through a world of glorious possibilities. And those of us that fall here are just as imaginative, but in a different sort of way.

Then there are those who have to imagine being imaginative. We have to work at it. Conjure it up. Constantly press the edges of our mind ever-outward in some herculean effort to go where our minds have never gone before. We're believers in the imaginative and we rest in the belief that what we see is the raw material from which to create what we don't see. We believe that life doesn't necessarily withhold grand visions from us, but it certainly doesn't hand them out freely either. We know the imagination to be something hard-won through the incessant exercise of creativity. There are times when seeking out something imaginative seems more akin to walking in an endless wasteland. And at other times it just flows in some sort of glorious cavalcade. But either way, we have to work at it.

We've All Got An Imagination

However we come about it and however we engage it, we all have a truly great imagination. A low self-esteem would tell us that we don't. Or if we do, it will say that we don't have the ability to access it, much less use it if we could get our hands on it. We must remember that an imagination is part of our DNA. It's part of the packaging. It's standard. It's not an accessory or an upgrade or that rare thing that shows up in the rarest of people. It's part of our basic design. And therefore, you have one and you likely have a great one.

What An Imagination Can Do

We're uniquely gifted with the ability to visualize something that doesn't exist and bring that hitherto nonexistent thing into the existence that it never had. Our minds are not restricted or held hostage to the realities that surround us. We are not bound to the suffocating parameters that would outwardly appear to be the impenetrable boundaries of some confining existence. We have the rather profound and even slightly romantic ability to see beyond the walls without even seeing over them. What 'is' only represents what could be. And while none of that is magic, sometimes it feels utterly magical.

Imaginations   grant   us   the   ability   to

mysteriously and rather decisively move beyond the confining parameters of our limited existence and visualize things that lie leagues outside that existence. Without an imagination we would be irreparably shackled to 'what is' and never be released to 'what could be.' Imagination allows us to blow out the boundaries of life out so far that life becomes a life without limits, a life of endless possibilities. It creates that wonderfully intriguing contradiction between what appears to be immovable as held against an imagination that moves everything.

Such is the power and such is the reach of our imaginations. The reality is that this is something that we all possess in abundance far beyond that which we realize. And if we could grasp that concept, we would feed hungry self-esteems, counter the horrible messages of inadequacy that they repeat to us, and raise our sense of self immeasurably. Maybe we could begin to imagine how great we are.

God and Our Imagination
Indeed, God has granted us a riotously expansive imagination packaged full of boundless creativity. Our imagination is our humanity cut loose. In the rawest essence of that imagination, we see something that's less of us and more of Him. It's extraordinarily difficult to figure out how something like our imaginations could be birthed from the raw stuff of the world that swirls around us. How could

the sum total of the existence that lays all around us possibly add up to the great imaginings that flow from within us? How could the raw materials be enough to explain the raw wonder of the things that we craft from them?

There must be something external that winds and wanders through our thoughts, and in the winding and the wandering raises up and weaves together something beyond the imagination of our imagination. Is it brilliance, or something more? Indeed, we are born dreamers with imaginations rogue and wonderful.

When we take a moment to consider the indecipherable inventiveness, the breath-taking breadth, the unfathomable depth, and the unexplainable creativity of our imaginations, we realize that the ingredients for such a thing are a gift of priceless proportions. It seems that our imaginations can transport us leagues beyond the realities around us. Therefore, we might consider that such a vehicle tells us that we have been gifted with the ability to enjoy the life around us, while being able to create a life beyond us. We can immerse ourselves in what 'is' while fashioning what is 'not.' Our imaginations seem to be one of those curious things that defy sufficient explanation unless they're explained by something we can't necessarily explain. And that immensity of the gift should speak to the immensity of our value.

Curiosity would prod me to postulate that our imagination is some slight sliver of the eternal strategically implanted within us at some key place. More specifically, I would suggest that it's a tiny shard of God's infinite genius and wholly immeasurable character that we have within us simply because we were created in God's image. Or to put it another way, it may well be that our imagination is a bit of God that's found its way into us by some genetic thread that runs back to creation itself, when God raised man up from the soil of a long last Garden that itself oozed with the fruit and prowess of God's imagination.

If we think about it, God has the greatest imagination in all of existence. Look around you. Who in the world could come up with the stuff that you walk by every day? My guess is that it came from the Someone Who created that world. The greatest imagination in all of existence is one that would be able to take 'nothing' and imagine the 'something' that we live in from 'nothing' from which it came. In fact, to fully imagine 'nothing' in the fullness of 'nothing' takes an imagination of proportions that our imaginations simply can't envision. Such is the magnitude and measure of God's imagination that He could imagine 'nothing,' and then bring all of creation out of all of 'nothing.' And could it be that we've got a thin thread (or possibly a woven tapestry of threads) of that within us ourselves? If so, our value cannot be underestimated.

Room to Run

If our imagination is a tiny inherited part of God intricately woven in the foundational fabric of our being, then the world around us would be completely insufficient to contain it. In other words, we'd quickly run out of running room. How do you create enough space for an imagination that's built to defy space? How do you make enough room for something that was meant to defy the very concept of 'room?'

Yet, God has set up a created order whose expanse will always exceed the reach of our imagination. As a manifestation of His creative genius God granted us sprawling imaginations, yet He gave us enough room so that those imaginations will never run out of room. He fashioned a created order that infinitely eclipsed the furthest boundaries that our imaginations could ever take us. In the beauty of it all, we can think beyond the parameters of ourselves, but never hit a wall beyond which nothing exists.

How valuable must we be that this God granted us this expansive imagination and then crafted the creation within which He placed us so that our imaginations would never run into a wall? He crafted an existence where our lives are not spent drearily calculating all of the endings that are always approaching and how we're going to manage them once they arrive. Rather, He crafted an existence that invites us to the beginnings that always ride hard on the heels of every ending.

Additionally, He created us in a manner that the place that our imaginations takes us sets the stage for the next place in some sort of glorious perpetual motion. Our imagination is not just about imagining what we're imagining at the moment that we're imagining it. Rather, what we're imagining today is the springboard for the thing that we'll be imagining tomorrow. The excitement of a new idea rolls over into the next idea in a nearly divine momentum that leaves us breathless in the anticipation of what's coming next. This unimaginable scenario is woven within each of us, rendering us full of a potential that is indeed unimaginable. And how much must God have loved us and cherished us with some wild abandon in order to put all of that in place for us? Indeed, it defies imagination and it evidences that we are better than we might have imagined ourselves to be.

The Greatest Thing to Imagine
It may be that one of the greatest functions of our imagination is to press our view of ourselves outside of the suffocating walls that we've placed around ourselves. Maybe our imagination is best served by imagining what we can be. Can we imagine that we are better? Can we imagine that what we are is far

greater than what we've come to believe that we are? Can we imagine that we've reined in ourselves based on tainted mistruths and toxic distortions that we've embraced as truth? Can we imagine that the sense of self that we've constructed is in fact a deconstructed self? Any of these would be a strikingly profound and wonderfully healing use of our imagination.

Is it possible that one of the greatest functions of this phenomenal gift is to imagine ourselves as better than we believe ourselves to be? More than that, can we imagine how God views us, for that would likely be the greatest exercise of our imagination? Can we imagine how He sees us? Can we imagine God shaping us in His heart and ordering our circumstances in a manner that 'what we are' would find 'who He is' in the most profound way possible? Can we then imagine that we are here for a purpose that is greater than our abilities and broader than the number of our years? That God placed us here not to bide our time, but change our world? Can we imagine things of this sort, because these are nothing of imagination but everything of fact?

Should this gift of imagination be pressed into the service of low self-esteems so that what we dare to imagine ourselves to be is in fact who we truly are? Could it be that what we can imagine about ourselves is not only what we can become, but what we already are? Can we imagine that it's not about reclaiming what we lost, but reclaiming the reality that it never left? It's my sense that maybe the most potent and providential use of this gift is to unleash it in the service of devastated self-esteems.

As we've noted, it's really quite amazing that we can utilize the fullest of our imaginations and never run out of room to imagine. Our imaginations can serve us for a lifetime and never come close to exhaustion. And as we've said, shouldn't they be used to lift our self-esteem in just such a fashion? I would suggest that our imagination is eternity working itself out right in the middle of our everyday doldrums, particularly those that beset us regarding our view of ourselves. Our imagination reveals the seemingly impossible reality that the prison doors were never locked. More than that, an imagination divulges the forever fact that there were never any locks in the first place.

Imagination and Our Faithlessness

Yet, quite often we see the limit of our imaginations as the limit of all that exists. We do that because we don't see ourselves as being capable of living out something that extensive and wildly stunning. If we can't imagine it, we often assume that it's not there to imagine. And sometimes it's safer not to imagine it because we don't see ourselves as capable of living it should we imagine it. We end up playing by the rules of our own imaginations which do indeed have limitations that are tightly reined in by our low sense of self. There are no locks, but somewhere we assume that they must be there. And these things may well be the most powerful limitations that bedevil us.

Indeed, it seems that our self-esteems rein in this richest of gifts. Our self-esteems pull in the impossible and tie down the stuff of dreams. They lead us to believe that real imaginations are for those who are gifted with the resources to take the stuff of imagination and weave it into the stuff of reality. Our low self-esteems temper our imaginations more than we likely imagine, eventually leaving us horribly emaciated and barely breathing.

It seems that we soothe ourselves by imagining that we have an imagination so as not to fall prey to the melancholy stagnation that flits and flirts all about us. But to be unleashed into something boldly imaginative or to have something that grand intersect our lives is seen as better than what we are, beyond our ability to manage and thereby suggests that we are inadequate to give it legs and let it run. And when we temper our imagination and press it into something that is more suited to our poor self-image it is no longer our imagination. Rather, it becomes something more like scantily clad ideas posturing as an imagination so that we might not let it loose.

Faith and Imagination

God freely functions both inside and outside of the limitations that we place on our imagination, as He is neither limited nor intimidated by either. When He functions within the parameters of our imaginations we appear to do quite well, for then it matches the limited estimation of ourselves. But when God functions outside of them, we are forced to accept that which we cannot conceptualize. And what we cannot conceptualize is that we possess a value equivalent to the place that God has taken us. Knowing that we would get stuck in such precarious places, God granted us the capacity for something that we call faith. And faith is being willing to imagine what we cannot see, so that we can do what we cannot imagine.

Faith is needed at the point where our imaginations stop and God keeps right on going. Faith says that there's more than we could ever imagine and we have sufficient value to inhabit those places. It says that despite the vastness of our imaginations, there's an infinity that lies beyond that vastness that we are privileged to experience. Faith says that there is a grand journey that was set in motion before we were born so that our lives would be warmed by the call of it from the day we were born until the day that we die. And to have all of that set in place without ever asking for it suggests our worth and God's love.

The existence of faith itself speaks to the reality of our limitations and the existence of something far bigger than our imaginations. It says that there's things that we simply won't be able to grasp, or conceptualize, or rationalize, or quantify, or explain, or imagine unless we simply take them by faith. Faith is a 'must' in an existence whose reality far supersedes our ability to conceptualize the vast majority of it. Faith is what's needed at the point that our imaginations reach that understanding. Faith says that the point that we are forced to stop because the limits of our imaginations have been expended is the point that God is just barely beginning. Faith unleashes us to believe that we have the right to imagine and the worth to go the place that we've imagined.

Faith as Imagination Unleashed

Faith is imagination fully unleashed. Faith is what takes us beyond the parameters of our imaginations and allows us to imagine beyond ourselves. Faith is where we lean on something else because leaning on our own imaginations has run out of gas. Faith is imagining what our imaginations cannot. It creates an infinite extension. It's what breaks us free to truly break out of the confines within which we live. Faith is God's way of taking the limitations of our humanity and allowing us the unimaginable privilege of crossing beyond them. Faith breaks the stranglehold that our damaged self-esteem has on us and causes us to believe that we are more. Faith then is a step in which we can touch the hem of God's imagination, be granted a vision beyond a vision and then be both informed and inspired to dream beyond our own dreams.

Imagine Faith

If we can't imagine faith as our imaginations unleashed, then we're not fully utilizing our imaginations. If we can imagine being limited, it's because we refused to embrace faith as the ultimate key to the ultimate imagination. And if we can begin to imagine an imagination cut loose by faith, then maybe we've actually begun to utilize what our imaginations were intended for in the first place. Imagine a life without boundaries. Imagine that you were cherished enough by God for Him to liberally grant you that imagination. Step out in faith in God and your imagination will go to places hitherto unimagined, for God deems you worthy of going there and capable of crafting it to the reality you've hoped it to be.

The Hard Questions:

1. What keeps you from having the ability to imagine yourself as better than you believe yourself to be?
2. Is that thing something that's true or is a distortion that you've come to believe? If you believe it's true, what evidence do you have to support it?
3. What steps would you have to take to begin to imagine yourself as better than you imagine yourself to be? What first step can you take to imagine

The Self That I Long to Believe In

yourself as God imagines you?

Chapter 14
The Soul of the Soul
Game Changers

"Then the LORD said to Moses, "Why are you crying out to me? Tell the Israelites to move on. Raise your staff and stretch out your hand over the sea to divide the water so that the Israelites can go through the sea on dry ground."
-    Exodus 14:15-16 (NIV)

"In a world full of game players, the only way to set yourself apart is to be a game changer."
-    Matshona Dhliwayo

There are those people who plumb the depths of their souls and press into the innermost caverns of their hearts. There are those most robust adventurers who realize that the greatest adventures of all don't lie without; rather they lie within. There are those who have come to the priceless realization that to effectively navigate the world is not to become the world, but to become the fullest self-living in the world. And these are the people that are the game changers.

These are the people who have moved past some exercise of self-discovery and have probed more deeply. These are the radical explorers. These are the individuals who stalwartly sit before God knowing that to sit there is be in the presence of the

One who created all the things about them that they are thirsty to discover. We are found in Him since He founded us. He holds our blueprint, and He crafted the calling that seamlessly fits that blueprint. He holds every question that we have about who we are. These are the people that realize that to find some sense of self is a commitment to a perpetual journey of self-discovery. And that begins with the God Who created us so that there might be the joy of discovery in the first place.

These are the people who refuse to get caught up in the world, but who refuse to ignore it as well. These are the people who engage the world to change it rather than just to survive it. They are human, so they become fatigued at times and the thought of surrender crosses their minds on darker days. Frustrations will chase hard after them and their internal insecurities will rise to mock their dreams. And if perchance they fall prey to lesser impulses, they will right themselves and set out yet again. These are the game-changers.

The Battle Turned Inward
Yes, we fought against all of those things that were outside of us, but we also fight against what they did to everything inside of us. We moved from fighting these forces to fighting the damage that they caused within us. In time, we were left attending to our many wounds because at times they became bigger than the battles that had inflicted them.

194

Additionally, we knew that to fight the next battles that were certain to come meant healing from the ones we'd just fought. And while the wounds from the previous battles are often our greatest point of inspiration for fighting the next battles, we must at some level heal. So, we turn inward.

We also turn inward because we find ourselves fighting against ourselves. As we've noted earlier, we are often our own worst enemy. Too often we're engaged in hand-to-hand combat against ourselves. In our better moments we're engaged in hand-holding-hand support as we lift ourselves up or speak words of encouragement in times of great distress. Or we're constantly running back inside of ourselves because the need inside has become greater than the battle raging outside.

It Does Not End on the Inside

As we come to understand who we are, we also begin to understand that while this journey begins with oneself, it hardly ends there. This internal vastness that continues to unfold and lay itself bare in front of us becomes more than us. God did not make us big enough to contain all that we are. We must move outside of ourselves or we will suffocate inside of ourselves. The lie of a low self-esteem is that we are small both inside and outside. That is nowhere in God's design even though it's everywhere in our head.

The Self That I Long to Believe In

In time, we begin to understand that the exploration of self is, in fact, performed in the service of others. While we thought this to be our own journey, it is in reality the journey of others. The battle within always has correlations to the world without. Nothing ends with us. What we fight inside of us will always have application to what's transpiring outside of us. There's someone out there whose life will be made complete by what we completed in our lives. There's a task out there that will be finalized only because we finalized the task in here. Battles will be won or lost based on what we brought to them because we fought them inside of ourselves first. We are not big enough to contain all that we are because the world needs all that we are. It needs the game-changer inside of us.

Therefore, we press out the boundaries, press in the conviction to always press out and we grow in ways that we thought impossible. We don't fear becoming more than what we can contain. Rather, we learn to revel in it and run in hot pursuit of it because we know that there is nothing to fear in becoming what God created us to be. The world is waiting for us to show up because we will show up with an armload of things that we never thought we possessed. And in that arduous yet marvelous process, we too become game-changers when we never imagined that we possessed the resources to do so.

This journey of self-discovery is not ours alone. We thought it to be so because we felt so isolated in it. It was us with us. Yes, we fought against the demands of the culture, the messages of those who sought to diminish us, the belittling roles that others forced upon us, as well as the baser decisions of others that all but killed us. Oh yes, we were challenged by emerging philosophies that fought against what we were fighting for and assailed us with an ever-increasing intensity as we began to be successful in the fight against them. But all of these were fought because the battles forming on the world's horizon needed us to be ready when these battles showed up.

Too Grand to Be Contained

Something so grand cannot be kept to itself. Of course we must attend to our wounds if we are to fight the battles. Of course we must take care of what's inside in order to effectively engage what's outside. But can we let attending to our wounds become 'the' battle? Can we make the needs of self the story of ourselves? For whatever reason that we do it, can we draw inside of ourselves (out of what might be a very legitimate rationale to heal and grow) and believe that that process will not eventually press us out of ourselves?

Too Grand to Be Contained for Too Long

There's a point where our journey becomes bigger than 'our' journey despite the wounds that we sustained in the journey. It becomes bigger than the battle that we're waging against ourselves or the efforts that we're putting forth to help ourselves. And that point typically comes a whole sooner than we think it should. We can readily acknowledge the need to take ourselves outside of ourselves, but we rarely feel ready when the time comes. It's always too soon. It's always premature. There's always a few things that aren't quite where they need to be or a few adjustments that are yet to be made. There's always something.

The fact that we don't feel ready evidences the fact that we are. For if we presume ourselves to be ready, we likewise assume that we're clear on what it takes to be ready. Instead, maybe being ready is understanding that we'll never totally understand what 'ready' is. Being ready likewise assumes that we can take on all (or most) of this massive venture on our own. And if we leave no room for God or if we leave the amount of room that we think is appropriate, we might become a game-changer but all of the games will of the smallest sort.

At some point before we are ready, the battle will move outside of us. And maybe more than that, it will move outside of us to the point that it will eventually move beyond us. It will become bigger than our ability to manage, but not bigger than our ability to commit to. We have the capacity for such things. We've always had the capacity. We are game-changers who are just waiting to be game-changers.

We Are Game-Changers
We were always game-changers, we just didn't know it. We hadn't called that side of ourselves up and out. It laid there in some dormant state, waiting to be awakened. This book has been about that awakening. That rousing from slumber. That nudge that stirs the sleeping giant within. But the awakening doesn't result in the realization. That comes in time. That comes as we gradually realize that we are more than ourselves. That we exceed what we need. And as that excess grows and as our awareness of it sharpens we begin asking what we're supposed to do with it.

It's hardly plausible to believe that it's just supposed to sit there. And it would be selfish to think that somehow it's this generous bonus that we're privileged to hold and savor for the rest of our lives. And as these realizations become clearer, we realize that we are here to change things. We are here to make a difference. The larger focus of all of this work is not us at all. In fact, it has very little to do with us. Rather, it has everything to do with everything around us.

There is then this growing assumption that the world 'within' is sufficiently vast to shape the world 'without.' That the size of the person is equal to the challenges of the world. That we have come equipped with an internal nature and a sufficient depth that when understood and subsequently brought to bear on the world is capable bending the shape of that world. That God designed us as game-changers even though we have fallen prey to the notion that we're not even invited to the game. And if we were to consider the vast capacity inherent within us by which worlds can be changed, and if we understand that God fully partners with those resources, we might find our poor self-esteem lifted if not eliminated. For if we have the capacity to change the course of a world running rogue, we can change the shape of ourselves as well.

The Size of Game-Changing

And these are the world-changers that we would be wise to admire, and to which we would be equally wise to aspire. These are who we are becoming. This is us becoming the 'us' that we've always been. We might be called to change something large or we might be called to change something small. It might be a few people or it might be a mass of people. It might be to change history or simply touch the moment. It might be nothing more than gently nudging the trajectory of something or it could be reversing the course of it entirely. It's not the size of the thing that we've been called to change, for size is irrelevant.

Size is something that our culture uses as a

measuring stick to determine the value of something. The bigger the thing, the greater the value. Not in God's economy. What's relevant is that we were called to it, we responded to the call and we did it. Big or small, we did it. And as we understand that we are the game-changers in whatever way God has called us to do that, we might consider what kind of game-changer we're going to be.

Game-Changers

The Thoughtful Rebels

I have been repeatedly impacted by many such thoughtful rebels. I have seen the many who build inward-out, rather than outward-in. There are those who daily stand in the gap and create the space for others to find out who they are so they're not told who they are. There are many who have challenged the norms, rejected the trends, stood firm when others fled and held the line on an intruding world so that those around them could be in the world, but not of the world. There are those wisely rogue people who run against the world in order to change the world.

They are a thoughtful bunch, which separates them sufficiently from the reactive crowd that would errantly bestow the label of 'rebel' upon themselves. These sorts of people recognize that a rebellion is of the heart. That it's a call to something great versus something different. They realize that the call can be to something that has been abandoned that never should have been abandoned, even if they were the ones that abandoned it. That aspiring to something does not mean that they were called to it. That a chorus of voices jointly raised in the support of something does not mean that it's a calling to those who are raising their voices, much less a calling to the game-changers. They are thoughtful. They are dreamers grounded by all things good that allow those dreams to become all things great.

When our self-esteem is low, our lives are not about being a thoughtful rebel simple because we are not sufficient for any cause. Yet, throughout this book I have worked to have us become thoughtful. Deeply thoughtful. Foundationally thoughtful. And if we apply the same thoughtfulness to the world around us that we have been prompted to apply to ourselves we are then positioned to change that world. We can become the thoughtful rebels. Self-esteem or not, we become game-changers.

Godly Game Changers
Game-changers must have a guiding force that keeps them true, straight and targeted on things of real value. They must not fall prey to selfish agendas or stray into lesser things. They must have strength of focus, a steeled character of unbridled morality, a fortitude to stay strong against the lure of a seductive culture and a commitment to not become entranced

by the emerging strength of themselves.

The bane of growing strong in a sinful world is that that world will fight against that growth unless it's wrestled into servitude to that world. There is little glory in changing a world that needs to be changed, but there is a whole lot of pain involved in it. There is struggle. There is sacrifice. There are moments of utter exhaustion and ice-cold desperation. The reality of sacrifice is the ingredient of change. We don't hold onto our lives as we seek to change others. Rather, we let go of our lives. Not in some sort of free-fall or death march. Not in some manner sacrificially irresponsible. But in a manner that releases enough of us into them so that enough of them is touched by enough of God.

And it is a relationship with God that perfectly positions all of these things, that keeps them in balance, that feeds them to keep them strong, and that shields us from everything that would rip us apart and wound the self-esteems we've spent so much time healing. God has been a game-changer since mankind changed the game by falling into sin. And He invites each of us to that task. It's the Godly game-changers that change today for an eternity that is little more than a blink away.

The Game-Changers
And these are the game-changers who were birthed by those who themselves first changed the game.

These are the movers and the shakers that walked in the footsteps of others who were constantly moving things and shaking what was left. These are astutely discerning people who understood the world, but differentiated themselves sufficiently from the world so as to not be shackled by norms, swayed by trends, bullied by fads, baffled by the mediocrity and capsized by the ever-changing currents of culture and societal expectations.

Many of these game-changers were game-changers because of others who refused to let them be anything else. I applaud those bold people, the fearless people, the sacrificial people who refused to bend to culture or trends so that their friends and children might grow into who they are, versus turning into what the world is. I can count innumerable men and women who created the space and ran interference at great cost to themselves to guide others who knew who they were, versus being children who were trying to figure out who the world was telling them that they are.

This is who you are called to be. This is your legacy. This is everything that your damaged self-esteem tells you that you're not, but it is in fact everything that you are. It is what we have been building toward throughout this book. It's about building our self-esteem in the pursuit of the calling that our self-esteem would never let us pursue. It's the unleashing within us of everything that should have never been leashed. It is become who you are in the most glorious way that you can become that person.

So who will we be? How will we live out our lives? Will we be what the world demands we be, or will we be what our soul encourages us to be and who God invites us to be? And in making those decisions, will we look beyond ourselves to create a space for others to do the same? Will we leave a legacy for the game-changers who will follow that will give them both the hope and the template to become the game-changers that they were destined to be?

The Hard Questions:
1. In what specific way could you be a game-changer?
2. What would be the first step (even if it's a small one) that you could take in becoming a game-changer?
3. What will you do to take that first step?

Chapter 15
Conclusion
To Paint

"When I look at your heavens, the work of your fingers, the moon and the stars, which you have set in place, what is man that you are mindful of him, and the son of man that you care for him?"
-    Psalm 8:3-5 (NIV)

"Whatever you see within yourself, let it be the whole of yourself. For too often we have been brutalized by our own sense of inadequacy and we've been held hostage to the lesser choices born of such a debilitating sense of self. Know this, that latent within you there lies more than ample resources begging to be called forth to smash the chains forged of such an incapacitating sense of self. And it is my prayer that you would press against everything within you that would hold you back, and that you would raise whatever voice you have and extend that call."
-    Craig D. Lounsbrough

This conclusion is not about a summation of what you've just read, for you're more than capable of going back and reviewing what was handed to you in the preceding pages. I prefer not to be redundant. Rather, I prefer to be inspirational.

Rather, much like the rest of this book the

conclusion is a call to something better than you believe yourself to be worthy of. It's not that we deserve a strong sense of self and a sturdy self-confidence. It's that we already have those resources within us and we likewise have more than adequate assets to build on those resources. We just haven't cultivated them because we haven't believed that they were there to be cultivated. In a sense, we just need to be awakened to who we are, not who we thought ourselves to be.

And so to close, I would like to close with a story that illustrates those points. A true story. A story that embodies so much of what I have tried to say in this book. A story that has stayed with me these many decades and one that I have shared frequently. A story of a shattered self-esteem raised strong and unleashed in a way that left a powerful legacy in the lives of many, including myself. A story of triumph. A story that's waiting to be your story.

I would encourage you to sit with this simple story and thereby let it sit with you. And in doing so, may the principles, thoughts and ideals outlined in this book be ever-more deeply pressed into the seams of your soul because of this one simple, obscure life that has impacted so many other lives.

Wendy's Painting – To Live Until We Die
She was scarcely nineteen when the doctor scanned the x-ray, turning it this way and that with an

unnerving sort of scrutiny that was horribly unsettling in a journey that had been unsettling long before its arrival in that room on that day. Sometimes it's the collecting and arranging of the words that evidences the gravity of them. The doctor was doing exactly that. Clipping the x-ray onto the stark florescent panel in front of her, he stepped back, removed his glasses, folded his arms, cleared his throat and spoke the death in the x-ray into the quietness of the room.

There are moments in life, rare as they are, that are weighted with enough force to imprudently redefine the whole of our lives for the rest of our lives. There are moments where we are left with no means by which to return to what was, despite the ever-pressing desperation to flee to those safer places. And in the selfsame manner, there is no escaping from what now will be, despite the foreboding dread of it. We tend to visualize these kinds of moments as tumultuous, loud and crushing. But sometimes these things are silent; horror arriving on tiptoe. Sometimes they're just an x-ray clipped onto a panel.

Death Arrives Early
The untrained eye doesn't need much preparation to see death when it's stalking a life, even a nineteen-year-old one. Death did not belong in the x-ray of someone so young, who had just barely charted the course of her future to abruptly realize that there

would be none. Despite the sudden blindness that trauma impertinently strikes us with, it remained unmistakable. Much like a thick, venomous snake wrapping its tensely muscular body around its victim in some sort of remorseless death roll, cancer had wrapped its dark death around the whole of her esophagus and had thrust pointed fingers deep into both of her lungs. Insidiously, cancer had secretly laid claim to a life that was only beginning to lay claim to her own life.

Her name was Wendy, and the mention of her name reminds me of the strength of this woman who herself was barely a woman. Sitting in the sterile waiting room only a few feet away from doctors and x-rays, I was about to share in a journey that would impact my own journey for the rest of time.

In that darkened room but a few scant steps away, with the black and misty gray shadows of the x-ray playing themselves back across her face, Wendy's world seized up and came to a jolting stop. The simple plastic clock on the far wall kept ticking away the seconds, for it did not realize that time might always move but sometimes life stops. For Wendy, it had stopped. Staring into the shades of gray and black, the entirety of her existence violently imploded, suddenly becoming the sum total of that one, muddled gray x-ray that silently screamed the awful reality. A life is more than one x-ray. But that day, it was not. The doctor took it down, held it for a moment, ushered in the nurse and walked away.

The Death in Trying to Live
Months of seemingly endless treatments passed. Nights twisted by the wrenching pain wrought of the convulsions that are left in the aftermath of chemotherapy's mad search for cancer. Hours lying prone on the surface of cold, heartless tables upon which she was strapped as lethal beams of invisible radiation were shot into her body, leaving her without hair and starkly skeletal from its cruel side effects.

Her life became the story of endless hours of tremors, deeply running chills that would not succumb to any blanket and days blurred to weeks and more in the gut-wrenching of uncontrolled vomiting. Whether waking or sleeping, she was incessantly taunted by the stalking specter of hopelessness, and she was chased to cliff's edge by a heartless helplessness. In time, the effort to save her became worse than the dying that she fought to avoid. Finally, the efforts of men played themselves out, placing her beyond the technology of men and at the mercy of cancer's dark death, its pointed fingers and a patiently awaiting God.

The Need of a Vision
We always need a vision. It lies deep in the essence of our subterranean being. But at times like this, it's

not about a vision to give us a sense that our life has meaning. Sometimes we are way past that. Rather, at times like this we need a vision to give us a sense that our death has purpose. And if our death has purpose, the life that led up to it has purpose as well. And when these most desperate of moments rise to a place where they now tread the crumbling escarpment of death itself, we need life to deliver a vision to us because we have long lost the strength to set out in search of one. There are few things that possess the capacity to hold the fullness of desperation as much as a pending death that has no vision to grant it purpose. But God will not let such moments stand.

The Delivering of a Vision

And so, in one remarkable moment, God used the ugliness of cancer to birth a vision in Wendy's life where there had been none. There is no place in any part of life where there is not a purpose. Purpose stands entirely distinct and forever erect despite the nature of the circumstances that stand poised around it. It exists eternally set apart from tragedy, misfortune, loss, injustices of the most grievous kind and attacks of the more horrendous sort. It is never diminished by the force of the emotions that arise from events that scream the meaninglessness of meaning not yet discovered. Never would God permit that to be so.

And therefore, in His loving and perfect

wisdom He laid His hand on her dying body not to heal it, but to place a picture in her mind that would birth a far, far greater healing. It was not a beautiful picture at all, but for Wendy it was the perfect picture. It was the image of the x-ray that had cast its gray shadows on her face and her life so many months earlier.

The Need of Color

Slowly, she began to see her world in that x-ray. Not the cancer that it revealed so profoundly, for that was far too insignificant. Rather, it was the color. Much like that x-ray, she saw her world as filled with misty grays and blotches of black. The x-ray had no depth, no vibrancy, no brilliant hues. She realized that a world without Christ was veiled with those very same hues and void of color altogether. Her life and that of the world around her was not something stolen by this disease. Rather, it was the disease that revealed to her how much sin had stolen from the world and how horribly gray it had left her and everything around her.

Wendy was an extraordinarily gifted artist, richly blessed with robust vision, boundless creativity and the genius to bring any vision to canvas. She realized that this gift had been given precisely for this moment, this time and this revelation that could only have been borne of the savagery of this time. At moments such as these a gift must be great, for only a great gift is able overcome such a great darkness and rise above such a brutal savagery. Only a great gift possesses sufficient tenderness, ample creativity, a sufficiently deep acumen and a restless passion that in unison are capable of putting the greatest vision to paper, or writing out a melody in flowing stanzas, or painting an awaiting canvas in broad relief when such an endeavor appeared impossible. And Wendy was gifted.

To Paint
Weak and horribly emaciated, she gathered her brushes, assembled her paints and pulled a weakening body up to an awaiting easel. With one arm rendered completely useless due to the prolonged bombardments of radiation, she took her one good arm, pressed against the pain and put her brushes to the canvas. Each agonizing stroke was filled with the compulsion to leave her world something of beauty, something that would lift out the brilliant colors that God has placed in her soul and splash them across the canvas so that they might leap off of it and splash its colors into the lives of those who would marvel at her work. To put to canvas the hope of a living color that would outlive her ability to speak it.

For those last two months she painted prolifically. She would exhaust herself seated among brushes, paints, an ever-patient easel and a relentless vision. Frequently pulling herself to a simple bed that sat but a few steps away, she would sleep for an hour or two and then place herself back in the middle of brushes, paints and vision. I often sat beside her as she created works of art that had a life to them that utterly defied the death that was quickly overtaking her. She painted in a prolific mix of rich colors and beautiful tones: sweeping, majestic and touched of the magic of a soul that has been touched by the heart of God. I sat and watched her pour into her paintings the very life force that was perpetually bleeding out of her.

The Color Never Dies
The last painting that she began was never finished. Although she somehow spent herself far beyond the reach of her own strength, Wendy was to succumb to the cold darkness of cancer before the piece was completed. It was a listlessly serene sketch of two Canada geese smoothly breaking the mirrored surface of a wooded lake. It was a painting that was full of potential, rich with possibility, and it captured in bold relief the persistence of a life so that it might speak life into the lives it would leave behind. However, it will never be finished. The life of the artist from which it sprung was spent before it could be given over to the painting.

Today this painting sits in my office, forever uncompleted as it should be. It reminds me of the millions of lives around me that are gray, lifeless and flat. Often, the deathly gray appearance of many of

214

the lives that we encounter would lead us to believe that there is no hope for color, or worse yet, that color does not exist at all. That the palette of every life is nothing but gray and black, being doomed to be forever so.

Yet, this unfinished painting reminds us that each of those lives is full of potential and rich with possibility just like that painting and the artist from whose soul it sprung. Each life is color waiting to happen. Everyone is color on the verge of a glorious explosion. And like that painting, every life sits among brushes, paints, an ever-patient easel and a relentless vision waiting to be completed. And may we seat ourselves there, invite others to sit beside us, take brush in hand and paint.

A Few Last Words
I hope that you take the words in this book and go paint. Paint a life of vitality. Of vibrant color. Of rich hues and deep tones. Paint a life that will encourage others to paint. Pick up your brush, pull the canvas close to you and, like Wendy, paint with everything in you. And once you've begun that, invite someone to sit with you and watch you paint. As they become inspired by what they see in you, hand them a brush or two, pull an empty canvas up in front of them and let them paint as well.

God has called you to paint. So go paint. Paint prolifically. Paint with great fervor and electric enthusiasm. Press your low self-esteem aside and paint anyway. Paint your life full of the color that you were designed to live with. Paint over all of the "black and misty gray shadows" within you that have served to define you for far too long. Do what you've been told you can't do and go paint.

For the world is changed when we change ourselves. The world is changed by believing in ourselves. The world is changed by unleashing ourselves because we have that belief. So, take the thoughts outlined in this book, massage their truths deep into the crevices of your soul, apply them to your life every day, and get painting.

CPSIA information can be obtained
at www.ICGtesting.com
Printed in the USA
FSHW010322230921
84925FS